One Planet,
One People

One Planet, One People

Beyond
"Us vs. Them"

Carl Coon
Former Ambassador to Nepal

Prometheus Books
59 John Glenn Drive
Amherst, New York 14228-2197

Published 2004 by Prometheus Books

Inquiries should be addressed to
Prometheus Books
59 John Glenn Drive
Amherst, New York 14228–2197
VOICE: 716–691–0133, ext. 207
FAX: 716–564–2711
WWW.PROMETHEUSBOOKS.COM

08 07 06 05 04   5 4 3 2 1

Library of Congress Cataloging-in-Publication Data

Coon, Carleton Stevens, 1927–
    One planet, one people : beyond "us. vs. them" / Carl Coon
        p. cm.
    ISBN 1–59102–233–9 (hardcover: alk. paper)
    1. Social evolution. 2. Social history. 3. Evolutionary psychology.
4. Internationalism. I. Title.

HM626.C66 2004
303.4—dc22

2004010428

Printed in the United States of America on acid-free paper

Contents

Foreword

I know few authors who would have dared to treat so wide a subject in a single volume—nothing less than the fifty-thousand-year history of human civilization—nor would they have succeeded so brilliantly in their chosen task.

Appropriately subtitled "Beyond 'Us vs. Them,'" this book traces the evolution of human culture through an ever-widening application of the principles of altruism: feelings, which in our primitive ancestors may have been entirely genetic in origin, but which have come to be applied through cultural evolution to an ever-widening circle of groups, tribes, and nations.

If all that Coon had achieved were a succinct survey of our human history it would be achievement enough. But he goes further and shows that just as human beings throughout history have had to learn to adapt and deal with ever larger and more divergent groups, so today we are on the threshold of one more such change—from a world of competing ideologies and nation-states to a world that can and must learn to accommodate diversity and live in peace and harmony. The new world order of Coon's vision will come about through stronger international institutions, increasing respect for the rule of law, and above all, through a universal acceptance of the autonomy of the individual and respect for human rights.

Carl Coon combines a breadth of vision and depth of understanding with a facility of expression that set him apart from most historians, anthropologists, and political commentators writing today. His lifetime of experience as a senior US diplomat has given him the perfect background from which to survey the present state of world politics. A must-read for every student and observer of today's rapidly changing political landscape.

Roy W. Brown
President, International Humanist and Ethical Union
Founder and former chair, World Population Foundation
Board member, International Foundation for
Population and Development

Preface

The other day a friend asked me what I was doing and I told him I was writing a book. "What for?" he asked. "Everybody's writing a book these days, and nobody has time to read them." He continued: "Can you honestly tell me that there is something truly original in your book, something that hasn't been hashed over in other books already in one form or another?" Tough question, I admitted, then tried an answer along the following lines:

"You take two broad areas of scholastic study, each populated with thousands of specialists, and examine the gray area in between. A risky business, because some specialist on one side or the other will know more than you do about anything you say, and nail you. But it can be done, it has been done, and the results are sometimes interesting and possibly even original."

"And what might those areas be?" asked my friend.

"The first," I replied, "is science, particularly anthropology and evolutionary psychology. The second is international politics, current affairs, modern diplomacy. And there's a third one, philosophy and religion, that kept knocking at my door and would not allow itself to be excluded."

"Hmph," said my friend, carefully signifying neither approval nor disapproval. (Like me, he was a retired diplomat.)

I have over thirty years' experience as a professional diplomat, plus an abiding interest in the diverse cultures I have come to know.

I have always had a strong interest in anthropology and human origins, no doubt resulting from growing up in the shadow of an exceptionally knowledgeable anthropologist father. I have never compartmentalized; I've always been interested in the interconnection between these two areas of human knowledge and experience. Slowly, over the years, what I've learned in each field has mellowed and shed light on the other. It is this interconnectedness, this perspective that each side sheds on the other, that is, in my opinion, unusual enough to merit this book.

Many friends have looked over early drafts of this book and offered helpful suggestions, including Joyce Abell, Louis Cabot, Ed Lovett, Frank Miele, Margaret Nydell, Suzanne Olds, and Matt Silliman. As the book progressed, I have benefited from thoughtful comment from leading humanists: Dr. Paul Kurtz, Tony Hileman, and Roy Brown. On the scientific side I have tapped many sources, as my footnotes will show, but I particularly wish to cite Dr. Peter J. Richerson of the University of California at Davis. Dr. Richerson has given me wise advice and counsel many times when I was struggling to pull together some of the central ideas of this book.

The political assessments and judgments about current conditions are, except as noted, based on my experiences as a diplomat. They taught me, among other things, how to compress a large body of complex material into a brief, readable form for the edification of busy superiors. Some of my friends have commented that this book is "very short." I take that as a compliment.

PEOPLE OF EARTH[*]

A Secular Hymn for the Next Millennium

People of Earth,
We reach for the stars,
But never forget,
That the Earth gave us birth.

Children of Earth
Your numbers were small
Your knowledge was slim
But you worshiped the Earth.

Everything changed,
Our numbers increased,
We worshiped false gods,
And we ravaged the Earth.

Now that we've grown
And know what we are
We love and respect
Our mother, the Earth.

People of Earth,
We reach for the stars,
But never forget
That the Earth gave us birth . . .
    Yes, the Earth gave us birth . . .
       Gave us birth . . .
          Gave . . . us . . . birth . . .

---

*Music and lyrics by Carl Coon

1.

Overview

This book is really two books, dealing with different subjects, and cobbled together by the fact that human societies grow over time and evolve in the general direction of greater complexity. The first "book" analyzes the process that governs how that evolution works, and traces its course, from the earliest humans to the rise of the nation-state. I have defined the principles that govern that process in my own way, drawing on recent theoretical work by evolutionary psychologists, anthropologists, and other scientists. The second "book" deals with the contemporary scene, and with the future. It is based on material readily available in the popular press, as I interpret it, using my past experience as a diplomat. My hope is that if we can discern a pattern in the first part, perhaps we can apply the principles we have distilled out of that study to the problems of the present era. We might even apply those principles to consideration of what kind of world we want to leave to our grandchildren.

Throughout this book I treat religion as one of several phenomena that have critically influenced the evolution of human societies. I look at it from the outside, as a scientist does, rather than from the inside, as an apologist or advocate. For this reason I doubt whether my argument will find much favor with religious fundamentalists. It is a scientific, Darwinian perspective, and I make no bones about it. People who believe in the literal truth of the Bible or the Qur'an have their own ideas about how humankind originated, and they are not going to be impressed by my explanations. I'm writing this book for the rest of us, whether we call ourselves atheists or humanists or followers of any of the traditional religious faiths. The only criterion is that the people in this group do not believe in miracles.

My central thesis is that the dawn of the third millennium finds humanity in the middle of a crucially important and difficult transition. Think of it as the second big bang of the human mind (with apologies to the cosmologists, for stealing their phrase). Our first big bang occurred about fifty thousand years ago, when our remote ancestors began to construct a complex world of verbal symbols. That transition started us on a course that separated us from all other life on our planet; I'll discuss it in more detail in chapter 8.

The second big bang had its roots in the energy and population explosion that began to manifest itself about a quarter of a millennium ago. Now we are right in the middle of it, and are developing machines that exponentially augment the capabilities of our biologically evolved brains. This seminal breakthrough will open vistas we cannot yet even imagine. We can, however, predict that the future can be a very bright and fulfilling one for our quarrelsome but adaptive species, if we can somehow resolve or work around a plethora of urgent and critical new problems and challenges.

These problems are the focus of the second part of the book. I review them generally, and in the specific context of the Bush administration's unilateralist approach to international relations. That approach stands out as a destructive aberration. It has not only been ethically bankrupt, it has proved unworkable except in the very short term. Chairman Mao's "Great Leap Forward" comes to mind, which set China back a generation. The United States should be leading the rest of the world toward a strengthened United Nations, rather than applying its enormous influence in the opposite direction.

Perhaps the most important conclusion to emerge from this study is that we are being forced by circumstances largely of our own making to work out new global institutions of governance. These will be sustainable only if backed by a new global ethic that subordinates our old loyalties—to nation, ethnic group, and religion—to a new sense of the essential unity of humankind. We need to understand why these old loyalties exist, and respect them for the roles they played in the evolution of modern societies. Then we can appreciate the value of human diversity, and gradually create a future world order that builds on that diversity, and allows full scope for those essential human qualities that have already made us such a remarkable species.

2.

Two Worlds

Modern scientific thinking rejects the old concept of dual worlds, the world of the spirit existing in parallel to that of the body. But everyone knows that not everything that exists in this world we inhabit is tangible, touchable, and tasteable. Aren't ideas real too? What are our thoughts? What is the conscious mind?

Our ancestors have probably been puzzling over the mystery of consciousness, one way or another, ever since they became capable of abstract thought. What is the real "me"? Is it nothing more than my material body? Isn't there some kind of essence that is nonmaterial? If not, how to explain consciousness, thinking, and all the other aspects of mental activity? If so, how to describe that nonmaterial essence that gives meaning to the self?

Recent explorations into the basic workings of the human brain have helped us think about the nature of human thought. By now, "Virtually all contemporary scientists and philosophers . . . agree that the mind, which comprises consciousness and rational process, is the brain at work."[1] This admirably concise statement does not answer all our questions, but at least it is a start. The human brain is just one more result of an evolutionary process, rather than having been consciously created by some superior intelligence or being. It happens to be an extraordinary offshoot of the evolutionary process, which developed from runaway selection into something quite different from anything else in the biosphere. Nevertheless, it evolved. It was not "created." That is the explanation that fits the facts as we have come to know them.

Well and good, the brain evolved. But what is the mind? How does a lump of gray custard inside somebody's head produce a scenario, a sonnet, a symphony? What's going on here, you ask the scientists? Here you are, explaining everything, from electrons to galaxies, but how do you explain my thoughts?

In order to answer that question, we need to remind ourselves that biological life began only when some extremely unlikely conditions obtained. Most of the universe, as far as we can tell, is inhospitable to life. Our planet had an unusual biosphere that allowed certain chemical reactions to occur. Increasingly complex molecules formed over time, and eventually produced something that was capable of replicating itself. Once replication started, the basis was laid for evolution, and life began to work its long and tortuous way up to the level of complexity we now see in the biological world around us—including the human brain.[2]

The human brain evolved because it conferred survival value on its owners, in the context of the environments in which those owners lived. It and other evolutionary changes made language possible. Our remote ancestors began to talk to each other, using symbols to represent objects and conditions in the world around them. Language increasingly separated humans from other primates. People could exchange their thoughts. Information could be passed from one person to another, and from one generation to another. Knowledge and techniques could be stored and recalled later on, as needed.

Eventually humans took another leap forward and began using verbal symbols to designate abstractions, concepts like loyalty and trust, right and wrong, body versus soul. When this happened, a new environment appeared on our planet, a world of ideas, creatures of the mind. This world rapidly became populated with a host of new creatures—techniques, art forms, humor, religion, ethical do's and dont's, and much else.

There is a loose analogy here to the birth of biological life. In each case, truly extraordinary circumstances created the essential preconditions for something spectacularly different to happen, involving replicating entities that could evolve and proliferate. When biological life began, something brand new in the solar system and perhaps even our galaxy was born. When the human brain evolved, something even more original, brand new in the solar system and probably even in our galaxy, was born.

Plato was right, in a sense. There *are* two worlds, two universes: the physical world around us, which includes biological life as well as the geophysical environment, and the world of the human mind. But he was wrong in saying the real one was the mental one. They are both real, equally real. They came about differently; the mental world had to wait a long time, after biological life began, for the right conditions to evolve. But then, biological life had to wait around even longer, for the right environmental conditions to occur before *it* could get started. We are what we are because we are the result of a series of extraordinarily uncommon coincidences. Who says we aren't special?

THE WORLDS ARE SEPARATE BUT INTERDEPENDENT

The biophysical world that exists objectively in the planet around us, and the mental one that we have created in our minds, are mutually dependent. Ever since the world of the mind was first created, it has carried on an intricate dance with the physical world, each strongly influencing the other. Our relatively new world of the mind is, of course, an outgrowth of the biophysical world and remains subject to limits imposed by that world and the laws that govern it. Human ingenuity, however, is gradually overcoming some of the more obvious physical constraints, including many that we used to take for granted.

For example, water does not normally run uphill. But people have invented ways of making water run uphill, and we do so whenever we turn on a faucet. Some physical plumbing is involved but the concepts and techniques that make this possible are part of our mental world. People have different physical appearances that are determined by the genes they inherited from their parents. Genetic replication is something that has been a feature of the biophysical world for a very long time, long before we came along and developed the world of the mind, so we can safely assign the physical features we inherit to the biophysical world. But when a woman uses mascara and lipstick she is altering her physical appearance, and her altered appearance, and the effect it has on others, is part of our mental world. In each of these cases certain physical changes occurred, but you have to look to the world of the human mind to understand why they occurred and what form they took.

This view, unlike old-fashioned dualism, is a logical outgrowth of the so-called naturalistic philosophy which largely replaced dualism, at least for the modern, scientifically oriented individual. The naturalist denies the existence of unexplainable deities and other phenomena traditionally associated with religions. That which matters is that which can be derived from the physical world, and verified. But once we start thinking about the occult, and God, and other supernatural phenomena as creatures invented, disseminated, and retained by human minds, the old arguments between the dualists and the monists become irrelevant. Does God exist? Certainly, in the minds of many people. Let us stop the sterile argument about whether God is real, and examine what forms God takes in different cultures, and reflect upon the reasons for the differences, and how they evolved over time. Why is it so important to so many people that the Shroud of Turin be "proven" to be an authentic relic of Jesus? Why do they go to such lengths to argue against the physical evidence that it is nothing more than a fourteenth-century fake?

In other words, it is becoming evident that the real argument is not so much over whether "God" *exists*. It is over the more tangible (and provable) argument of whether "God" or some other occult force can intervene directly in the physical world we inhabit. Here the naturalists are on solid ground, for every effort by the true believers to demonstrate the "reality" of God's acts, by adducing direct intervention in the form of, say, miracles, has failed the test of rigorous scientific analysis.

There is still a huge argument raging among philosophers about the so-called naturalistic fallacy. The old-fashioned dualists were upset by naturalistic theories because they said that if there is no morality in nature per se, then how can humans act in ethical ways? You cannot derive an "ought" from an "is," was their most famous and quotable phrase. But surely, if you accept the reality of the world of human constructs, you can see how ethical principles not only can be a part of that world, but indeed can be an essential element of it. The fact of the matter is, the world of the human mind requires not just one mind, but many if it is to develop and flourish. If many minds are to live in reasonably cooperative social groups, something has to be in place that keeps the majority of the individuals cooperating. And that "something," first and foremost, is ethics.

NOTES

1. Edward O. Wilson, *Consilience: The Unity of Knowledge* (New York: Knopf, 1998), pp. 107–108.

2. John Maynard Smith and Eörs Szathmáry, *The Origins of Life: From the Birth of Life to the Origin of Language* (New York: Oxford University Press, 1999).

3.

Creatures of the Mind

Imagine a huge arboretum, with all kinds of trees and bushes and other plants growing in profusion. Populate it with all manner of animal life, from small insects to large mammals. And then, flip the whole thing over into a kind of jungle where each living creature, both animal and vegetable, is part of that world of human thoughts I describe in the last chapter. Instead of small buzzing insects one finds one-liner jokes, and tunes from the latest hits. Instead of squirrels and field mice, one hears the latest catchy phrases, slang that the kids are repeating to each other. Instead of flowers along the way, one sees the latest fashions in dresses. Instead of large herbivores, one hears the ponderous phrases of the talking heads on television, reaffirming current conventional wisdom. And then there are the predators, the carnivores, stalking the unwary consumer in a host of advertisements. Finally, there are huge trees, some of them centuries in the making. These are the basic ethical guidelines, the philosophical and religious beliefs that shape our entire life view.

As this somewhat labored analogy suggests, the variety of mental constructs in our human world today is rich and diverse, comparable in complexity to the biological world around us. And while there are differences between the ways the two worlds operate, there are also some important similarities.

- Creatures of the mind, like creatures of the earth, are born and grow up and get old and die. But there are many different kinds of these mental creatures, and they vary widely in fundamental respects, including longevity, mass, and geographical distribution.
- Climate zones have characteristic clusters of plants and animals. Each organism has adapted to the zone it inhabits in its own way, and settled into a harmonious and often symbiotic relation with its neighbors. Likewise, creatures of the mind are usually found in clusters; some such agglomerations are sometimes referred to as cultures, while others are identified as religions.
- There is a process of natural selection at work, for concepts compete for space in human minds, and that space, for better or worse, is never infinite, even in the most retentive brains.

Several years ago I had the good fortune to visit the forest of Bialowiecza in eastern Poland. It is the only substantial tract of genuinely virgin forest in all of Europe. And what a difference! As I walked through it, accompanied by an able guide, I saw a bewildering variety of plant forms that had specialized and adapted to imperceptible variations in soil, proximity to water, microclimatology, and other variables. Over thousands of years, natural selection had operated at increasingly subtle levels, with each refinement opening up the possibility of still more highly specialized ones. There are thousands of plant species in Bialowiecza that simply do not exist anyplace else. No other temperate forest I've ever seen could match its variety. It was like the Library of Congress compared to your corner book store. It gave new meaning to the term "climax vegetation."

Was the climax vegetation in Bialowiecza in a true state of equilibrium? Had it "arrived" and reached a degree of perfection beyond which further change, further adaptation was inconceivable? Of course not. There is no such thing as absolute perfection in our biosphere. Climax vegetation signifies a condition where natural selection has run its course for a long time under stable environmental conditions, where the rate of change has slowed down, and where the changes that do take place have moved from the macro to the micro level. In the modern era, examples of climax vegetation are rare; the norm is for rapidly changing environments that stress existing life forms and demand correspondingly high rates of adaptive change.

Can the concept of "climax vegetation" be applied to human societies? Perhaps it can apply to an era of protracted stability, during which a mature civilization proceeds from one generation to the next without major challenges, and where there is time for manners and morals to evolve that enable the society to function in a seamlessly cooperative and functional manner. Perhaps the Middle Kingdom under the pharaohs, or other empires where a single dynasty ruled for centuries, could be examples. But how would we know, from our own experience? Our world is more like a forest that some logging company clear-cut a few years back. A few scraggly trees in inaccessible spots, a bunch of saplings competing for future greatness, some wildflowers, and a vast plethora of weeds. The world of the human mind at the present time is certainly diverse and extensive, but it is not in the least settled or stable. The old verities have been uprooted, and instead of an orderly array of concepts that guide the individual's relation to the larger society, there is a vast wasteland of competing values and theories.

There are other ways we can use the analogy between the biological world and our mental constructs. Take the rough correlation between size and longevity. A fruit fly is gone tomorrow, but an elephant can live a hundred years, and a redwood even longer. One can infer a similar correlation for creatures of the mind. A joke that flashes across the Internet soon vanishes, except for a kind of fossil record in old e-mail files, to be replaced by others of its kind. Beethoven's *Eroica* symphony has endured for a couple of hundred years and is still in its prime. The Golden Rule has been around forever.

Our minds absorb the little creatures easily and soon discard them, but the real heavyweights in our mental world stay with us. For the most part we learn them as small children, and keep them until we die. These old oaks and redwoods in the jungles of our minds are the core beliefs that keep us functioning as members of our group. They are what we transmit to our children and grand-children, to provide continuity and ensure the perpetuation of the accumulated wisdom of prior generations. They are the building blocks of our personal ethical standards, informing us as to who is in our group and who isn't, and what is good and what isn't, and what is right and what is wrong. A significant part of our present distress is due to the fact that many of these old-growth trees have been cut down, and have yet to be replaced.

The great verities that we do learn as children, like the surviving oaks in our moral wasteland, are alive and growing, but they change only slowly. It is a basic aspect of human nature that we find it very hard to unlearn these verities, and replace them with ideas more suited to the times. When the pressure for change is great, the children adapt more rapidly than their elders. In the United States and other countries that have high levels of immigration, we see this principle operating. The parents never lose their accents and Old Country values, but their children assimilate. Since changes in basic values occur so slowly, when adaptive pressures are great, whole societies can become stressed. Does this sound familiar?

The spatial distribution of creatures of the mind is also some-what analogous to the geographic distribution of living organisms. Cultures often correlate with specific natural environments, or at least they can be traced back to origins that did. Religions can usually be considered in terms of the territory where they have many adherents, for example, the World of Islam, which stretches from North Africa to Indonesia.

ANALOGIES CAN ALSO BE MISLEADING

Living things replicate themselves, usually by sexual recombination of two sets of chromosomes, each containing many genes. This recombination produces a new array of genes that stays with the organism throughout its life. Ideas transmit differently. One mind communicates a concept to another mind, or perhaps several or more minds at once. The recipients pick it up and retain it for a while, and then some of them may pass it on. The original concept is influenced by the process of transmission; indeed, it may be fundamentally altered by the time it has passed through even a limited series of minds. The element of continuity that genes provide for living things is missing. Molecular biology has no parallel in the realm of ideas, and as far as we know it never will.

This means, among other things, that ideas can evolve far faster than biological organisms. In technical parlance, evolution is Lamarckian rather than Mendelian. Creatures of the mind don't need to wait around to adapt to new circumstances through a selection process that can take many generations. Some kinds of ideas evolve and even mutate in days or weeks. One generation of humans is more than enough to allow for adaptation through selection of almost (but not quite) all kinds of concepts.

There is another important difference between the two worlds. Our minds observe the physical world and think about it consciously; our survival depends on our doing so. It has always seemed entirely natural for us to think about material phenomena, to classify them, and to correlate our observations. That's what our brains evolved to do. Thinking about our mental world is a different matter. It can seem a bit like waking up from a dream. For fifty thousand years the consciousness of our ancestors has been focused on "things" not "thoughts." Until modern science came along, speculation about *how* and *why* we think has been limited and unsatisfactory. Now that we have a growing array of new tools, however, the philosophers are getting together with the scientists, and given our boundless curiosity, it is safe to predict that a new science of the mind will be a growth industry for a long time to come.[1]

Meanwhile, as of the date of this writing, we even lack a consensus about a generic name for the mental constructs that populate this world of ideas. I'm thinking about an analogue for the word "thing." The word "meme" has come to the fore during the past decade,[2] but different authorities use it in different ways, and it has by no means established itself as the term we are looking for.[3]

To sum up, there is a world of mental constructs that have a kind of life of their own, and evolve over time through a process of natural selection. It is evident that the ties that bind human societies together consist largely of creatures of the mind, not creatures of the earth. This is the foundation for our further analysis, in which we shall look at the societies themselves and how they are structured. In particular, we shall examine some of the principles that govern how they adapt to changing circumstances, and then trace the history of their evolution from simple bands to our increasingly integrated system of nation-states.

NOTES

1. "Spreading Consciousness," *Science News* 162, no. 16 (October 19, 2002): 251, summarizes recent findings of the neuroscientists and the controversies surrounding them, with philosophers joining the fray.

2. Richard Dawkins introduced the term "meme" in his now-classic *The Selfish Gene* (New York: Oxford University Press, 1989). It has been picked up by other scholars, notably Sue Blackmore (*The Meme Machine* [New York: Oxford University Press, 1999]).

3. See, for example, "The Selfish Meme," by William C. Wimsatt, in the November 2002 issue of *Natural History*.

4.

The Evolution of Complex Human Societies

No man (or woman) is an island. As we all know, we are social animals. Our ancestors, even those who lived before our earliest human ancestors, were social animals, and nothing in our evolutionary history has bent us in the direction of becoming a species of loners. On the contrary, the circumstances of our evolutionary history have impelled us in the direction of greater sociality, not less. Our long evolution over the last 150,000 years can be measured in terms of the gradual emergence of attitudes and institutions that have allowed ever larger groups of individuals to cooperate and function as members of a single society. It isn't physical or biological evolution that has made us what we are today, it is the evolution of complex societies. And that evolution has proceeded largely in the realm of the creatures of the mind described in the last two chapters. Modern societies are held together by steel frames which are made out of that subset of mental constructs that we know as behavioral principles. Those steel frames didn't get created all at once. No single architect designed them. Without exception, they evolved slowly and painfully. They represent the accumulated wisdom of many generations of our forebears. Ethical structures grow like a coral reef; modern societies all over the world are still adding to them.

WHAT IS A "SOCIETY"?

A society can be broadly defined as a group of individuals who sense that they form a community that is distinct from other communities, and separates them from outsiders. The "us versus them" syndrome is an essential element of this picture. This definition can be applied to any size group, from a basketball team to all humanity. I use the term in the narrower sense of describing those groups, and only those groups, to which the members attach their primary loyalty.

In 1945, while World War II was still being fought, I turned eighteen and was drafted into the US Army. I didn't want to go, as I was fully occupied as a student and didn't want to be taken away either from my university or from my family. But it never occurred to me to resist, for loyalty to my country trumped my ties to family and college. If asked what I was, I would automatically reply, I am an American.

About twenty years later, when I was posted in Tabriz, Iran, as US consul, I was circling the southern end of Lake Rezaiyeh outside the town of Miandoab. I happened to stop, and was instantly surrounded by a passel of local urchins who chattered to each other in their local patois. I asked something, I forget what, that implied I thought they were Turkish-speaking Iranian Azerbaijanis. The tallest boy looked at me scornfully and declared in ringing tones: "Kurdi" ("I am Kurdish!"). There was no question about his sense of identity. And it was not Iranian, though technically, in the eyes of the law, he was as much a citizen of Iran as I was of the United States. He was, first and foremost, a member of a society defined by Kurdish language and culture. That, not Iran, was the society he identified with.

This sense of group identity is central to the way humans organize into social units. The "us versus them" syndrome is a foundational element of human nature; it assumes that you treat other members of the in-group differently from outsiders. The difference between being a murderer or a wartime hero depends on whether the person you kill is part of your group or not. Cooperation between individuals within the group is regulated by ethical norms and by whatever coercive measures are available. Cooperation between groups is not similarly assured, unless the groups themselves are part of a higher level of social organization. Absent such a higher level, relations between groups can vary widely, ranging from friendly and cooperative to hostile and prone to conflict.[1]

How do behavioral guidelines evolve within a society, and how does that evolutionary process lead, sometimes, to the appearance of a more complex level of social organization comprising a number of formerly autonomous societies? The question is analogous to asking when and how an amoeba grows, and when and why it splits.

SEEKING A MORE PERFECT FIT
WITHIN A STATIC ENVIRONMENT

In the last chapter I discussed the forest at Bialowiecza, where organic life had been allowed to evolve for millennia within a stable and undisturbed environment. The evolutionary process was still going on, but the major problems had been solved, and adaptation was proceeding only at the micro level. As I noted, one can draw an analogy here to a stable society, where neither the physical nor the social environment changes very much over a span of many generations. When this idyllic situation obtains, people have time to work out ways to minimize the tensions between individual needs and the interests of the society as a whole. The process involves experimentation with different approaches, followed by a selection process and by general agreement on the best one. That approach or solution becomes enshrined in the perceived wisdom of the group, which is passed to children by their elders as part of the traditional values of that particular society. Those values constitute a kind of interlocking structure of behavioral guidelines, of do's and don'ts that allow the society to function as a cooperating entity despite the pull on individuals of selfish desires that, if unchecked, would undermine the group's integrity. People observe good manners as defined by the group because they were brought up that way, not because there is a policeman standing behind them all the time making them do so. They are honest in dealing with neighbors, and at least try to be kind to them, because they were brought up to believe this kind of behavior is right.

When ethics are allowed to evolve under stable circumstances, the usual result is a society where people don't need to be coerced to behave in ways that are in everyone's best interests. They act in socially responsible ways because they believe it is right. Protocol and etiquette become precisely defined. It's a harmonious society, but not a particularly creative one. Most people are conservative, and frown on anyone who rocks the boat.

When external circumstances threaten the society, the progression toward ever-increasing refinements in the ethical structure is slowed down or reversed. The group's most talented individuals address the new challenges, and leave the microtuning to more pedestrian minds. Creativity becomes more acceptable, at least for a while. The society changes more rapidly.

PRESSURES THAT FORCE MAJOR CHANGE

What sorts of major new challenges have human societies faced during their long evolution? In the earliest times, before our human ancestors developed societies more complex than hunter-gatherer bands, the sources of stress that required people to question and perhaps modify their behavioral patterns were mostly natural rather than self-induced. Perhaps the climate suddenly got colder (there were abrupt climatic swings during much of the Pleistocene), and people either learned to dress more warmly, or froze. More likely, a successful group would expand in numbers that eventually exceeded the locally available food supply. Some of them would move to another region and would have to adapt to a somewhat different environment when they got there. Rarely, bands without any prior history of contact would come together, and perhaps come into conflict.

After the introduction of agriculture, a lot of the earth's land surface that had been relatively unpopulated filled up with people, and different groups found themselves constantly bumping against each other. Competition for land increased. Conflict between societies became more the norm than the exception, and forced changes in the values and behavioral patterns of all concerned.

Quite recently, our unprecedented success as a species has forced us into an entirely new mode: managers of the planet, not just exploiters of whatever resources we were able to lay our hands on. This has forced us to start thinking about brand-new ethical structures, behavioral guidelines our ancestors never imagined. Act 3 in the drama of human adaptation is just beginning.

THE NUTS AND BOLTS OF SOCIAL EVOLUTION: WORKAROUNDS AND SPANDRELS

I know someone who likes corn on the cob, but cannot nibble the kernels like most people, because his front teeth are missing. So he takes a knife and cuts the kernels off the cob, then spoons them into his mouth and eats them that way. He has developed a procedure that solves a problem.

In the United States and most other countries, motor vehicles drive on the right. This is a procedure that has been worked out to address the problem that when there are a lot of automobiles on the road, they tend to bump into each other if there are no agreed-upon rules of the road.

Anthropologists Peter Richerson and Robert Boyd have coined the term "workarounds" to describe specific social mechanisms that develop within any society and help it avoid or overcome problems that get in the way of cooperation and the smooth functioning of the whole group.[2] These workarounds frequently take the form of ethical guidelines. Some of them are simple "don'ts" that restrain specific egoistic impulses, like "don't kill your neighbor" or "don't drive when drunk." Others are more general, like the ones that require respect for authority in hierarchical societies. Every culture has its own interlocking web of such rules, and they change over time as people adapt to a changing environment.

There can be conflicts between workarounds that require another layer of workarounds to resolve. To take a classic example, a hunter-gatherer male in a village-sized band has a primary obligation to feed his family. (Feeding his family is one of the most basic workarounds, reconciling the hunter's self-interest with the need to ensure that his genes pass on to future generations.) If he goes off by himself to hunt a rabbit, the chances are his family will eat meat fairly often. If he joins a drive hunt for big game, his chances of making a kill himself are sharply reduced, but someone will probably make a kill and there will be enough to go around. In some environments the second strategy may have a much better payoff for the group as a whole. Under such circumstances, an ethical guideline is needed that makes the individual hunter cooperate with other hunters, overriding his more basic ethical impulse to look first to the needs of his wife and children. Such an ethic will become a part of the total cultural behavior patterns that are drummed into children at an early age, and fortified afterward by peer-group pressure.

In the case at hand, the workaround has to involve more than simply instructing individual hunters to hunt collectively. There have to be rules as to who gets how much of the meat after a kill. After all, there's not much evolutionary benefit in hunting collectively if the hunters kill each other off squabbling over who gets which cut. In all the contemporary hunting societies we know where the hunters work collectively, there are quite specific, often elaborate, rules as to the sharing of the meat.[3] These may involve notions of hierarchy, and feeding specialists not directly engaged in the hunt, like shamans or flint knappers. In other words, the logic of hunting in groups may lead to collateral results which open up avenues for further adaptations. The late Stephen Jay Gould referred to these kinds of collateral results as "spandrels."[4]

Spandrels and workarounds interact in a complex manner, producing an intricate web of factors that produce adaptive changes. The rules governing hierarchy and specialization that facilitated big hunts weren't just spinoffs from the survival advantages of a new strategy to ensure better food supplies. They also represented workarounds for other problems our hunter-gatherer ancestors faced. Sexual selection probably played as big a role in producing hierarchies and specialists as the need to ensure food supplies.

It is difficult, and usually fruitless, to try to trace adaptive cultural breakthroughs to a single cause. When such breakthroughs happen, for whatever combination of reasons, they either work or they don't. If they work, they become a part of the ethical structures that regulate interpersonal behavior within that particular society or group. This kind of evolution resembles biological evolution in that it's on a ratchet. It only proceeds in one direction, barring some catastrophe that destroys the integrity of the group.

Symbolic thinking, as we shall see in chapter 8, was a massive breakthrough that shattered the old limits on the maximum size of a social group. In making possible a new kind of society, however, it created whole new clusters of ethical conflicts. Religion can be seen as a complex set of workarounds that came into its own following this transition. It not only provided a sense of belonging to a large community of coreligionists, but it spawned scores of spandrels that interacted with other workarounds and their spandrels to produce such diverse human activities as music and philosophy.

Yes, music and philosophy are more likely to have originated as spandrels than as workarounds, as did art, poetry, and other examples of the more complex excursions of the human mind. They were all ricochet effects rather than direct workarounds when they started. Human creativity is an accident; it was never foreordained.[5]

DIFFERENTIAL RATES OF CHANGE

As we saw in the last chapter, different kinds of mental constructs have different life spans. The most durable ones are the basic ethical workarounds that any society, however small or large, must have if it is to maintain some degree of cohesion. Essentially these involve variations of the Golden Rule. You treat your neighbor decently and expect he or she will reciprocate. Paul Kurtz defines these as the "common moral decencies,"[6] in which he includes personal integrity, trustworthiness, benevolence, and fairness. Some individuals in all societies follow these guidelines more rigorously than others, and some societies insist on this kind of behavior more rigorously than others, but they constitute standards which are respected in every coherent society, even when they are not followed.

Then there are the ethical principles each society has worked out somewhere along its own evolutionary track, which are important for holding that society together even though they may differ from comparable rules in other societies. The clusters of workarounds and spandrels we call religion fall into this category. They usually reiterate and reinforce the basic human decencies, while adding their own special rules, prohibitions, or requirements. For example: don't eat pork, be nice to cows, cross yourself on certain kinds of occasions, or visit Mecca once in your lifetime if you possibly can. These guidelines may seem unnecessary and even silly to outsiders, but they reinforce group identity and solidarity. As long as the individuals that comprise the society continue to attach a high value to their membership, these add-on rules are likely to persist.

Improvements in technology, as we know, are readily accepted when individuals perceive them as being useful, and as long they are not seen as threatening their "way of life," i.e., the ethical values central to their culture. But such improvements are often subversive, in that they introduce spandrels that can eventually undermine the "faith" of the people in the verities they were taught to believe. Every society has its inner conflicts between modernizing and conservative forces, our own being an outstanding example. It is religion for the most part that acts as a brake or balance wheel, in slowing down the rate of change of any society's values. There are no doubt evolutionary reasons for this, relating to the interplay between adaptability and continuity and the way the balance between them affects the survivability of human societies.

ETHICS VERSUS COERCION

Individuals who exploit other people in their group, and don't reciprocate, can destroy the solidarity of any society if they are allowed to pursue their selfish ends for long. There are two general approaches for managing this cheater problem: through ethical precepts that almost everyone accepts, and through external means of coercion. A society that relies primarily on general acceptance of appropriate ethical principles to maintain internal solidarity is likely to be more harmonious, happy, and functional than one that requires extensive instruments of coercion to keep people in line. In the village-sized groups of earlier times, the ancient, largely instinctive codes of behavior were enough to hold the group together, but that was only because everyone knew everyone else and malefactors could be quickly identified. In larger, more inclusive societies, more elaborate rules for behavior are needed, and usually they have to be backed up by coercive mechanisms.

It is probably fair to say that for a very long time now the pursuit of happiness in any society can be summed up as an effort to secure general accord on ethical principles that meet the requirements of the times well enough so that the need for coercive mechanisms is minimized. In fact, one can arrive at an operationally useful definition of good and evil in terms of behaviors and situations that push the balance one way or another. Almost any social system more elaborate than a kin-based band, if it is to survive, has to find a balance between a generally accepted code of ethics and mechanisms of coercion. A lot of the less admirable aspects of human history, from secular and religious tyranny to capitalist exploitation, can be explained in terms of ethical structures that have not caught up with the changing needs of the times, leaving a gap that can only be filled by coercion.

In the last chapter we drew an analogy between a biological environment that had reached the level of climax vegetation, and a society that had had many generations of stability in which to work out its internal stresses through the gradual evolution of ethical standards that had proven themselves effective as workarounds. Such a society sounds idyllic to us, looking at it from the perspective of our uncommonly turbulent era. It would certainly have the advantage that it wouldn't need many lawyers. But it probably wouldn't need a patent office either.

NOTES

1. In private correspondence, Dr. Peter J. Richerson, University of California, Davis, has commented: ". . . attitudes towards other groups vary enormously. Some . . . are admired and are not targets of hostility. Good and bad evaluations of other groups are usually but not always reciprocated. . . . The Blackfeet were allied with the Sarsis and the Sans Arcs, but were hereditary enemies of the Shoshone. . . ." Reprinted by permission of Peter J. Richerson.

2. Peter J. Richerson and Robert Boyd, "Complex Societies: The Evolutionary Origins of a Crude Superorganism," *Human Nature: An Interdisciplinary Biosocial Perspective* 10, no. 3 (1999): 253–89.

3. C. S. Coon, *The Hunting Peoples* (New York: N. Lyons Books, 1987), pp. 176–80. The rules as to how the meat will be shared vary a great deal from one group to another, but the principle of codifying how one shares is very common.

4. Stephen J. Gould and R. C. Lewontin, "The Spandrels of San Marco and the Panglossian Program: A Critique of the Adaptationist Programme," *Proceedings of the Royal Society of London* B205 (1979): 581–98.

5. Geoffrey F. Miller, *The Mating Mind: How Sexual Choice Shaped the Evolution of Human Nature* (New York: Doubleday, 2000), esp. chaps. 5 and 10; also Steven J. Mithen, *The Prehistory of the Mind: A Search for the Origins of Art, Religion, and Science* (London: Thames and Hudson, 1996), esp. chap. 9.

6. Paul Kurtz, *Forbidden Fruit: The Ethics of Humanism* (Amherst, NY: Prometheus Books, 1988). For a summary, see *Free Inquiry* (Winter 2002/2003): 5–6.

5.

The Problem of Altruism

Biologists, anthropologists, and other scientists define altruism as behavior that adds to the fitness of others at some cost to the fitness of the donor. They have long been troubled by the fact that many living things, especially human beings, act altruistically. Why should this be, if all that matters is fitness, and passing the pattern of the genes on to succeeding generations? If the whole process of evolutionary change is based on the selective survival of the more fit, why hasn't altruism been bred out of life in general?

The old-fashioned answer, the one that preceded the development of genetics, was that altruism within a group added to the fitness of the group as a whole, and when the group competed against other groups, this advantage helped it prevail. But as our knowledge of genetics increased, it became evident that biological inheritance could not transpire on a group basis, for genetic information is transmitted only through individuals. Natural selection between individuals within a group was normal, but natural selection between groups as a whole was considered a logical impossibility. By about 1960 the whole principle of group selection was generally discredited.[1] Not only was group selection rejected for other animals, it was rejected for humans as well. In an overzealous attempt to be consistent, the anthropologists joined the biologists and threw the baby out with the bathwater.

When group selection as an explanatory theory was rejected, other rather ingenious explanations were developed to explain the apparent paradox that altruistic behavior sometimes crops up in a "survival of the fittest" world. The first such theory was based on kinship, or genetic similarity. A mother bear protects her cubs, even at risk to herself, to make sure her own genetic message as replicated in her cubs will survive. Siblings, since they share a good deal of the same genetic message, may act altruistically toward each other for similar reasons. This kind of altruistic behavior can actually survive in a purely Darwinian world to the extent that the donor's sacrifice can improve the odds that shared genes will survive and be passed on.

Kin-based altruism appealed to scientists in that it could be tested empirically. Many studies have shown that, indeed, the propensity of an individual to act altruistically toward kin is normally greatest when the blood relationship is closest, and diminishes as the relationship becomes more distant. We already know this, of course, for it is conventional wisdom. But now we "know" it in a different sense, as scientifically "proven."

A second important contribution to the study of altruism during this period came to be known as "reciprocal altruism." You may help your neighbor, even at some cost, if you and that individual belong to a community where everyone knows everyone else, so that your act will be noted and, most likely, reciprocated. In a larger society where a freeloader can take your help and vanish into the woodwork, a system based on reciprocal altruism will not evolve.[2]

Here, as in the kin-based theory, scientists developed complex mathematical formulas and devised ingenious practical experiments that buttressed elaborations of the basic idea. Once again, we found the scientists developing complicated ways to prove empirically what everybody already knows, namely that life in a small community where everyone knows everyone else can be a lot simpler and easier on the nerves than life in a big city where one constantly deals with strangers.

The problem with these two theories is not that they are wrong; indeed, they offer rather convincing explanations for the natural evolution of altruistic behavior in nonhuman animals. (And I shall use them for part of my argument about human altruism in later parts of this book.) Their problem is that, especially for humans, they don't go far enough. Even combined, they present an implausibly austere view of human nature. Can we only act altruistically toward kin when our genes tell us to, and toward our neighbors when we know that directly or indirectly, we'll get paid back? Where is genuine affection and a desire to help someone else just because we want to, even if there is no possibility of compensation? How can people feel compassion for perfect strangers? Where is there room in this picture of human nature for that mysterious thing called love?

There are still a lot of anthropologists and evolutionary biologists who answer these questions by saying that it may look like love, but if you plumb the emotional depths, it's really only egoism in disguise. And they buttress this view by reciting their mantra that selection cannot operate between groups, only through individuals—and individuals are destined by the laws of evolution to be egoists. But this view is going out of fashion, at least as far as cultural selection between human groups is concerned. A recent book coauthored by a biologist (David Sloane Wilson) and a philosopher (Elliott Sober)[3] makes a persuasive case that in human societies, selection occurs at both the individual and the group levels. In fact, they say, human social evolution results from a highly complex interaction between the two. On the individual level, the principle of selection for fitness operates in favor of selfish behavior, while at the group level the fitness factor works the other way, encouraging genuine altruism.

This sounds a bit complicated, but the principle becomes clearer when we step back from how humans evolve, and look at an example from how humans help domestic animals evolve, through selective breeding. Sober and Wilson cite the case of US commercial chicken farmers. For many generations, farmers picked the hens that laid the most eggs and used them for breeding stock. Pretty soon egg production failed to improve and in some cases went down. Then some genius, who had not heard that group selection was an invalid theory, broke the birds up into groups and took the most successful *groups* for breeding stock, without trying to differentiate which chickens within the groups were doing the best. "Annual egg production increased 160 percent in only 6 generations." It seems that harmonious groups of our favorite fowl do better than groups of prima donnas, who apparently tend to be unpleasant to their neighbors and get in each other's way. The authors conclude that once the egg industry catches on to this scientifically frowned-on approach, ". . . the projected annual savings will far exceed the money spent by the U.S. government for basic research in evolutionary biology."[4]

What's going on here? Is it possible that a whole generation of learned scientists have missed the boat in this basic aspect of evolutionary theory? It seems to me that that is precisely what has happened! The emperor has no clothes, and group selection is alive and well, along with pure altruism, despite what the peer group says. I am grateful to Sober and Wilson for publishing their unorthodox views in time for me to incorporate them in this effort to make sense of an issue that until recently has been thoroughly snarled up in wrong thinking.[5]

One purpose of this book is to analyze ethical principles in terms of their functions and how they evolve, rather than the usual approach of telling people how they ought to behave. I've had to clear away a lot of underbrush, from the dualism/naturalism debate to the notion that there is no such thing as group selection. Now let us get back to ethics, and look at them from the outside.

Any system of ethics is a set of behavioral guidelines aimed at maximizing cooperation and minimizing conflicts within a given group of people. Based foursquare on altruism, it evolves through group selection and serves as the basic antidote to the fissiparous pressures of individual egoism that evolve naturally through selection at the individual level. Egoism and altruism are the two poles between which all our human urges and constraints play their roles. They are the goalposts that define the playing field, the yin and yang of human nature.

Animals other than people can sometimes display altruism but don't have ethics. An individual in isolation (if there be such) doesn't need ethics. But groups of people do, because survival depends not only on individual fitness but on how well its members cooperate. We are different from other animals in that we have developed altruism into flexible and complex structures, which have enabled us to develop and inhabit a world of concepts rivaling the biophysical world in its diversity. The principles underlying these structures have evolved, allowing the concept of altruism to extend to ever larger groups. By making cooperation possible on larger scales they have made civilization as we know it possible.

CONCLUSION

The conceptual tools described in the last chapter can explain how complex human societies evolve. Altruism, as described here, tells us how they hold together. Now we can study social evolution more chronologically. To this end, we need to identify when major evolutionary advances occurred that allowed our ancestors to include substantially larger numbers of people in the societies to which they attached their primary loyalties. In other words, when and how did adaptations begin that fundamentally altered the size of the in-group? When and how did the "us versus them" syndrome morph into something new?

NOTES

1. George C. Williams, *Adaptation and Natural Selection: A Critique of Some Current Evolutionary Thought* (Princeton, NJ: Princeton University Press, 1966).

2. Matt Ridley, *The Origins of Virtue* (New York: Viking, 1996).

3. Elliott Sober and David Sloane Wilson, *Unto Others: The Evolution and Psychology of Unselfish Behavior* (Cambridge, MA: Harvard University Press, 1998).

4. Ibid., pp. 121–23.

5. The late Stephen Jay Gould discusses this mistaken dogma that group selection has no place in evolutionary theory in his magnum opus, *The Structure of Evolutionary Theory* (Cambridge, MA: Harvard University Press, 2002). See, for example, pp. 552–54.

6.

Finding the Joints

Wě constantly try to make the world around us more under-standable by chopping it up and labeling the pieces. Visible light comes in a continuous spectrum but we see it in terms of colors. We file letters according to whatever system we believe offers the best chance of retrieving them later. Any librarian understands the importance of a good system of classification. Any biologist understands the weaknesses as well as the strengths of the conventions commonly used to classify living things.

When we look back through time and around in space, we see a continuous spectrum of human societies, from the small and simple to the large and complex. The historical record makes it clear that this variety wasn't all created at the same time, but rather that it evolved. The technology needed to build a modern automobile didn't just spring out of nowhere, it developed gradually, piece by piece. The same is true of the patterns of human specialization and cooperation that make it possible to buy a car and maintain it, and have highways to drive it on.

Humans evolved biologically over a period spanning millions of years. We are still evolving, but the pace of biological evolution remains very slow, in relation to the kinds of change with which we are familiar. Within about the last hundred thousand years a new pattern of evolution has appeared, the evolution of human societies. This mainly involves changes in our cultures, not our genes.

This kind of change has been accelerating and is now happening orders of magnitude faster than biological evolution.

How can we classify the chronological stages of this process of cultural change? A century ago, anthropologists and historians often talked about three stages of social evolution: *savagery* phasing into *barbarism* phasing into *civilization.* This was a simplistic view, barely satisfactory then, and not at all helpful today. We need an approach that is less ethnocentric and more scientific.

This progression from small and simple human societies to large and complex ones follows certain rules. A given social group's size and complexity is a function of two important variables: the technological level the group has reached, and the capacity of the land it inhabits to provide the necessary resources at that particular technological level. In the remote past, all our ancestors lived at a technological level where the only sources of power available to them were fire and their own muscle. They grouped themselves, as we shall see, into small kin-based bands. If various things had not happened to rock the boat, we'd still be living that way. But things did happen, and now we live in multicultural megastates groping toward the establishment of a world community.

The developments that brought us rather jerkily into our present complexities were not, with rare exceptions, natural events—though climate change, for one thing, did play a part. Most of the changes our ancestors brought on themselves, sometimes by moving to a new area requiring creative adaptation to new circumstances, more often through copying some other group's changes.

Throughout recorded history, groups tended to remain fairly static for many generations, then lurch into some new configuration in a relatively brief timespan. We have no reason to believe it was otherwise with our prehistoric forebears, whose history will never be known in any detail, because it was unrecorded. The situation loosely resembles Stephen Jay Gould's "punctuated equilibrium" theory, which observes that biological evolution has, throughout geological time, occurred in fits and starts, not on a steady curve.

This is relevant to our task of deciding on a way to classify the stages of human social evolution. If the progression from simple to complex were a straight-line projection over time, any such classification would be pretty artificial and would likely prove of little help. But if there really are moments in time when the rate of change temporarily accelerated, we have something solid to work with.

When you carve a turkey it helps to know where the joints are. What are the most important "joints" in the long advance of our ancestors, from simple protohuman primates living in small bands, to our present large and complex societies?

Scientific investigations during the past century have given us a great deal of material to work with. Some of it is archeological, based on fossilized bones and flints and some understanding of climate shifts gleaned from geology. Some is based on extensive anthropological research on simple tribal groups that still exist in isolated regions. Both genetic and linguistic studies shed additional light. Finally, we have observations about our own society, its historical roots, and the new kinds of problems it faces. Historians, sociologists, political scientists, and economists, among others, have supplied data and analysis in such overwhelming amounts that no one can sift through it all.

It is, however, possible to arrive at an overview that combines the essence of all these sources. My efforts to this end suggest that there are certain "joints" or periods when where something happened that led to massive changes in human society. In between were longer periods when change was relatively slow and incremental. In each case, these longer periods were marked by an effective upper limit on the size and complexity of the social groupings into which our ancestors were organized.

What constitutes such an upper limit? Which factors, for example, prevented kin-based bands from organizing tribal confederations for millions of years? Or kept wandering tribes from organizing kingdoms for many millennia? Or are keeping modern nation-states, right now, from organizing a world government? There are many possible explanations, many theories, and some of them can usefully contribute to our understanding. There is one concept, however, that I favor, because it leads me most directly to a perception of where these "joints" can be found. That concept is our old friend altruism, the willing acceptance of obligations toward other members of your group. You cooperate with the group you have been brought up to regard as your own people. You are capable of altruistic behavior, sacrificing your immediate interests to help other members of the group. You assume, both instinctively and as a matter of common sense, that when everyone within the group cooperates, everyone benefits.

It comes down to a matter of trust. We all have an "us versus them" instinct which makes us want to distinguish between members of our group and outsiders. This is the essence of what it is to be a social animal; our remote ancestors had it long before they became human. Once our ancestors evolved into humans, this instinct for belonging to a group made possible the evolution of ethical constraints on individual egoistic behavior. Such behavioral rules, once they had been accepted as part of the culture of a group, could be learned in childhood. They built on and added new dimensions to the "hard-wired" rules built into our genes, which had evolved over much longer periods of time through biological evolution. Since they could change much faster than the rules we inherited, they added enormously to the adaptability of our species.

Ethics can be defined as behavioral guidelines generally accepted and observed by members of a group. A central thesis of this book is that our contemporary ethical precepts can be analyzed in terms of layers, corresponding to the periods between the major transitions that periodically enabled our ancestors to expand their sense of "in-group" to larger social units. One analogy might be a building with several stories, each built upon and resting on the one below it. Or think of it as an ever-expanding set of boxes. The cycle begins when a few of our forebears start to think outside the box of the culture they were raised in. They create a new and larger framework, but it takes many generations for the full potential of the new attitudes to be realized. The eventual result is a larger box, and in due course the cycle starts anew.

Important transitions happen when an unusual combination of circumstances encourages individuals to behave in ways which allow the concept of trust, or altruism, to extend to a much larger group.

When such changes occur, people normally change their behavior for proximate reasons, with the long-term benefit from cooperating on a new and larger scale arriving only as a collateral, unforeseen bonus. But once the changes have occurred, and have been accepted by the majority of the newly expanded group, the benefits of cooperation on the expanded scale become so compelling that reversion to the old patterns becomes totally unacceptable. Like biological evolution, this kind of long-term cultural change is on a ratchet.

This helps us understand why human societies have evolved stepwise rather than in a strictly linear fashion. The major transition points mark where the size, shape, and rules of the game have been fundamentally altered. Competition between the teams is muddled for a while until people sort matters out and get some notion of how to play the new game. Then there is a long period of competition during which first some teams, then others, appear in the lead. Toynbee's concept of the rise and fall of empires applies within this cycle, not to the cycle as a whole. Finally, the mold is broken, and the cycle starts over.

The most important transitions or "joints" are very rare. I would judge that there are only three of the first order of magnitude: when we first became physically modern humans, when we began to think like humans, and now. There are, of course, many intermediate transitions, and we shall consider some the more important ones. However, they are more like mileposts along the way than points at which we have changed our essence—or are in the process of doing so.

7.

On Kin and Community

The next several chapters deal with different stages in the evolution of human societies, from small hunter-gatherer bands to the future world community. We shall concentrate on exploring transitions, and on how and why each stage endured for a while and then phased into the next. The key factor, as we indicated in the last chapter, will be the maximum size of the social group within which the individual felt that he or she belonged—the "us versus them" factor.

We start where early humans began, with small, kin-based bands of perhaps twenty or thirty individuals. How were these bands structured, in terms of their social organization, and what were the unwritten rules that kept them together and cooperating? We must be careful to avoid the trap of drawing parallels with hunter-gatherer societies that still exist in places like the Amazon headwaters or the highlands of New Guinea. All these people, though they look primitive to us, are modern in that they have distinctive cultures. Culture is a human invention. If we are looking for the soil from which it grew, we have to go farther back. The best place to start is with our primate cousins, especially the chimpanzees.

Chimpanzees are more closely related to humans than any other species. Genetic studies suggest that we shared a common ancestor with chimps as recently as five million years ago, and that since then, we have changed physically far more than the chimps have. It is, therefore, reasonable to assume that we can gain at least an approximate idea of the social structure of our remote ancestors, at the time the genus *Homo* first branched off, by studying the behavior of modern chimps in their natural habitats.

Chimpanzees live in tightly knit communities that normally include twenty or thirty individuals. The social structure is based on male kin-bonding, i.e., the nucleus is a group of related males, with females generally imported from other bands.[1] The males dominate, with an alpha male enjoying priority in social status and access to females.[2] Raiding parties of young males from one troop will frequently poach on the territory of another troop, and kill when they find an isolated individual.[3] While attitudes toward chimps from other bands are generally hostile, within the band there is mutually beneficial cooperation. Males form stable alliances within the band; they hunt together and groom each other. Females share food and cooperate in other ways. "All members of the group are aware of who is allied to whom, and that conflict with one individual may lead to conflict with an entire coalition."[4] In other words, an element of reciprocal altruism has evolved in chimpanzees to supplement the in-group altruism that evolved from kinship ties.

The climate changed in parts of central Africa about five million years ago; some jungles were replaced by savannah, and our ancestors became bipedal walkers rather than tree-climbers like the chimp cousins they left behind. This new kind of primate evolved along several different lines, one of which led to *Homo erectus* and eventually *Homo sapiens.* Gradually the brain increased in size, as a consequence of the new lifestyle, the ability to walk upright, and other factors.

The evolution of erect posture and a larger brain influenced social behavior, because eventually females had more trouble in giving birth than before. The evolutionary answer to this problem was that the gestation period became reduced. It didn't get shorter in a chronological sense, but in the sense that birth occurred sooner in the total period between conception and the child's ability to fend for itself. A baby chimp matures much faster than a human;[5] the period when it still needs parental care, feeding, and protection ends much earlier in its life cycle. But with humans, the infant requires many years of parental care, or its survival chances are sharply reduced. The mother cannot do the whole job unassisted without risking her own survival prospects, let alone her chances of reproducing again in a reasonable period. The first and most obvious source of help is the father, since his genes are involved just as much as the mother's are. The evolutionary odds, therefore, tilted in favor of what the scientists call "male paternal investment." In other words, monogamy was reinvented, which largely (but not entirely) supplanted the sexual free-for-all of the chimps. (I say "reinvented" because certain other species had already become monogamous in response to different environmental pressures.)

Studies of other primates suggest that there is a correlation between brain size (relative to total body mass) and the size of the social group.[6] It makes sense that dealing regularly with larger numbers of individuals requires more mental effort than carrying on with a more limited number. Maybe that's one reason why the cranial capacities of our remote ancestors went up substantially in the relatively short period of several million years, since we left our chimpanzee cousins behind. Switching from an arboreal life to hunting and foraging in a savannah probably put a premium on cooperation by larger groups. This suggests that during that long period before our ancestors became anatomically modern humans, their bands or tribes were initially quite small, including perhaps twenty or thirty individuals like the chimps, but as the millennia rolled by, and cranial capacities increased, the groups got larger. Eventually, when the first fully fledged humans appeared on the scene, our expensive new brains had the capacity to manage interpersonal relations within still larger groups.

Meanwhile, anatomical changes associated with erect posture and brain size were making it possible to vocalize a wide range of sounds. The stage was set for the evolution of language. But what did the first language sound like? When did our ancestors acquire it? If, as Noam Chomsky has demonstrated, we all have a "universal grammar module" programmed into our gray cells as part of our genetic inheritance, did we come by it all at once or gradually? Biologists, anthropologists, linguists, and other scientists are still arguing about these issues, but finally, out of the froth of controversy, the outlines of an answer are coming into focus. Here is how I interpret the results of the argument.

There is an inherited special capacity for language that is unique to our species. It probably began to develop in rudimentary form several million years ago, and evolved gradually in tandem with the increasing size of the brain.[7] The first anatomically modern humans probably had at least a limited language capacity. And for the next several score thousands of years, up to the period of the Middle/Upper Paleolithic transition, this capacity played an increasingly important role in strengthening solidarity within the band.

Language changed the rules of the evolutionary game. It put a new twist on sexual selection. The alpha male chimp had his pick of the available females, or at least he got first crack at them, and he didn't have to be a poet or a diplomat to achieve that status. He simply had to be big enough and tough enough to whip the competition if and when another male was bold enough to challenge him. When humans began to talk, skill at managing interpersonal relations through verbal promises, flattery, and threats became an important indicator of status. So did the ability to plan and lead hunts that involved a team of males. High status thus was conferred not on the brawniest male, but on the cleverest and most articulate. Women meanwhile developed their own verbal skills, and displayed varying degrees of verbal proficiency. Each gender came to regard verbal skills in the other sex as indicators of fitness. Language evolved rapidly under the forced draft influence of both natural selection for fitness and sexual selection pressures.

To sum up: our early human ancestors were monogamous primates with at least the rudiments of language. When they first appeared on the scene, their largest social organization was probably a band held together by the genetic workings of kin-based altruism, with the beginnings of cooperation based on reciprocal altruism. They were very conservative by our standards, in the sense that technological innovation, as judged by the implements they left behind, was virtually nonexistent over hundreds of generations. They were probably conservative in their social patterns as well.

The first archeological evidence of anatomically modern humans dates back about 150,000 years. The transition to the Upper Paleolithic, to be described in the next chapter, occurred some fifty thousand years ago. We have very little knowledge of what went on during the roughly one hundred thousand years in between, but can hazard some informed guesses. Groups that used language more effectively probably fared better than others, because they could obtain food from the land more efficiently and were better at maintaining internal cohesion. So language proved efficient at the group selection level as well as the individual level within the group. We can see the beginning here of that symbiotic combination of egoistic evolution at the individual level, and increased collective fitness at the group level, that produced such rapid evolutionary change in the human condition once culture was up and running.

During this incubation period, the size of in-groups must have increased. But there were limits to how large social units could grow. For one thing, people were necessarily few and far between, even in favored areas, because their technology was so limited. Hunting and gathering techniques available in that period didn't yield enough food to support more than a minimal population.

A second limiting factor is inherent in the way the reciprocal altruism system works. Unless it is backed up by some enforcement system, designed to catch and punish cheaters, it breaks down when the social unit gets too big for everyone to know everyone else. How big is too big may vary with circumstances, but the essential criterion is that when you see somebody, you not only recognize his physical features, but you already know something about him. The Shire, where Frodo the Hobbit started his epic adventures in *Lord of the Rings*, is an idyllic representation of the kind of community where everybody knows everybody else and life is harmonious because nobody cheats, or gets away with it for long.

The social organization of our remote human ancestors probably varied quite a bit with time and place, but we can fairly confidently assume that the maximum size of the in-group was not appreciably bigger than Frodo's Shire. It could have consisted of small bands foraging independently but associating for collective activities like hunts for large mammals, or a larger, village-sized group remaining together as a cohesive unit. Presumably, as hunter-gatherers, they did not settle into permanent villages like their descendants did after the introduction of agriculture. But nevertheless, I shall, for convenience, use the term "village" to describe this level of social organization in the rest of this book.

There has not been much research, as far as I know, on the question of how many other individuals the average human can recognize as someone he or she "knows," as opposed to someone perceived as a stranger or outsider. As I have noted, there seems to be some correlation between brain size and this limit. As our brains got bigger, the number of people we could recognize as members of our own tribe or in-group got larger too. This number was probably around 30 to 50 for our chimp-like early ancestors, but by the time anatomically modern humans appeared, the number may have increased to around 150.[8]

Does this mean we cannot get to know more than 150 individuals? Does it mean we cannot associate ourselves with larger groups? Obviously, the common sense answer to both questions is resoundingly negative. But this does not negate the presumption that during that long predawn era before our human ancestors learned to think the way we do, they normally did not associate in larger groups. If so, our contemporary social instincts should reflect that long period during which most of the essential elements of our human nature were forged. In fact, the instinctive preference for associating with a limited number of individuals is very much part of our contemporary nature, and shows up in what might be called the comfort level of our lives. We *can* associate with larger numbers of people, and often *do*, but that involves learned behavior, not our social instincts, and it is more work.

In a village-sized community, the sense of belonging is a precious thing, to be guarded zealously. Interpersonal relations are self-regulating, through the seamless operation of reciprocal altruism. The fact that everyone knows everyone else provides a sense of security and comfort. Cooperation for the benefit of the group as a whole comes naturally, without pressure or intimidation. Time and time again, this sense of group solidarity must have made the difference between survival and extinction, during the long predawn era before our ancestors began to think like we do. It became a core element of our genetic endowment, of our human nature.

One of the distinguishing features of a village-sized social group, as opposed to larger units, is that just about everything people discuss with each other is rich in context. You don't need a whole lot of words to convey fairly subtle ideas, when the listener can be assumed to start with much the same background knowledge as the person doing the talking. And if we further assume that much of what people talk about in a village environment is each other, then it is possible to postulate that a desire to gossip was a major factor in developing the human capacity for language. I am reminded of one of Ellsworth Bunker's laconic Vermont village tales, about a farmer who brought his plow to the village blacksmith for repair:[9]

Blacksmith: "I see you broke yer plow."
Farmer: "Nope."
Blacksmith: "Must be your hired hand broke it."
Farmer: "Ayeh."
Blacksmith: "Same feller as got yer daughter in trouble, ain't it?"
Farmer: "Ayeh."
Blacksmith: "Clumsy, ain't he?"

Our early ancestors may not have been much good at expressing abstract concepts verbally, but within their limited linguistic capabilities, and through nonverbal behavior, they must have evolved many of the social rules and values that continue to inform us, even today. For example, when our ancestors began to choose mates for life, rather than couple randomly when the spirit moved them, and to select them for their brains as well as their brawn, perhaps we can identify the origins of the human emotion we call love. Similarly, didn't that period see the birth of qualities like loyalty, friendship, and admiration for others, based on respect rather than fear? I do believe that people were capable of feeling these kinds of human emotions well before they had the vocabulary to think about them in the abstract. And quite clearly, those emotions from their very beginning must have been directed primarily at other members of the community, not at outsiders.

There is an important conclusion we can draw from all of this. The finer points of the ethical rules modern men and women follow have been learned, as a part of whatever culture the individual is born into. But they are based on something that goes to the heart of human nature, namely the genetic rules for social behavior that our remote ancestors evolved over many tens of thousands of years, before they started to think conceptually, the way we do. The learned parts of our ethical structures can be unlearned and replaced if necessary, but the basic part is fixed, not negotiable. We are all, basically, social animals, and this requires us to behave in certain ways towards our neighbors, or suffer consequences. The Golden Rule goes way back. What has changed over the passage of time is not the principle, but the way the individual defines the group or groups of people to whom it applies.

NOTES

1. John Maynard Smith and Eörs Szathmáry, *The Origins of Life: From the Birth of Life to the Origin of Language* (New York: Oxford University Press, 1999), p. 141.

2. Carl Sagan and Ann Druyan, *Shadows of Forgotten Ancestors: A Search for Who We Are* (New York: Random House, 1992).

3. Richard Wrangham and Dale Peterson, *Demonic Males: Apes and the Origins of Human Violence* (Boston: Houghton Mifflin, 1996).

4. Robin Dunbar, Chris Knight, and Camilla Power, eds., *The Evolution of Culture: An Interdisciplinary View* (New Brunswick, NJ: Rutgers University Press, 1999).

5. Robert Wright, *The Moral Animal: The New Science of Evolutionary Psychology* (New York: Pantheon Books, 1994), p. 38.

6. Steven Mithen, *The Prehistory of the Mind: A Search for the Origins of Art, Religion, and Science* (London: Thames and Hudson, 1996), pp. 106–107.

7. Terrence W. Deacon, *The Symbolic Species: The Co-evolution of Language and the Brain* (New York: Norton, 1997). See also Steven Pinker, *The Language Instinct* (New York: W. Morrow and Co., 1994), chap. 11, pp. 332–69.

8. Mithen, *The Prehistory of the Mind*, esp. pp. 133–34 and footnotes. See also Dunbar, Knight, and Power, *The Evolution of Culture*, pp. 180–81.

9. I heard this directly from the source.

8.

Symbolism, the First Big Bang of the Human Mind

The scene is somewhere in East Africa or the Levant, and the time is about fifty thousand years ago. The cast consists of humans who were like us physically, but whose minds still operated only at a primitive level. Very slowly, very gradually by our standards, they had developed a capacity for language that was qualitatively different from the communication skills of other primates. They had learned to use tools more proficiently than other animals, and they had developed efficient patterns of social organization within groups small enough so that everyone knew everybody else. For about one hundred thousand years their forebears had been slowly developing along these lines, while the siblings and cousins of these forebears had explored and thinly populated most of the habitable parts of the Old World. But the mental world of these remote ancestors was still limited largely to thinking by association with objects, individuals, and events that they sensed directly from the biophysical world around them. They were conservative, like other animals, doing what they had learned to do as children, and not much more. The men made hand axes and hunted the same way their ancestors had; the women foraged for food the way their mothers had taught them. They courted each other and gossiped about each other, but only within the group. Outsiders were aliens, to be treated with suspicion and great caution, or even with hostility.

Then something happened that permanently changed the way

our species thought. It was mental rather than physical. It involved using the same genes, the same physical equipment, in new and different ways. We discovered a new way of thinking, based on attaching verbal labels to abstract concepts. We learned to imagine. It was like the bursting of a bubble. The Promethean characters in our drama, whom we could perfectly well call Adam and Eve, stepped outside the box that limited their ancestral thought patterns and started creating a whole new world of thought. That second reality, the world of the mind I have described in chapters 2 and 3, burst out of its cocoon and began to spread its new wings.

The scientists call it the "Middle/Upper Paleolithic transition," or simply the "Upper Paleolithic transition." Since neither version is exactly catchy, I'll use a shorthand version more suited to the truly revolutionary implications of that transitional period, and refer to it as the "Symbolic Revolution." People had language before it occurred, and language consists of symbols, but the whole process of thinking symbolically was revolutionized during the transition we are describing here, since for the first time, symbols were used on a large scale to create a new world populated by creatures of the mind.

The fact that this revolution took place is indisputable, given the archeological evidence. This record consists of the remains of ritual burials, jewelry, complex tools of flint and bone, and of course the famous cave paintings in France and elsewhere. Almost without exception these remains have been dated as falling within an era that began only about fifty thousand years ago.[1] Their relatively sudden emergence and their widespread occurrence suggest a society that burst its old bonds and was no longer bound to tradition in the way that earlier modern humans had been. Ritual burial implies the beginning of a sense of wonder at human immortality; complex tools imply a new capacity to imagine how a given job can be performed more efficiently, without having to learn it by rote from someone who already knew it; and the cave paintings demonstrate an ability to sit quietly in a private place and imagine what animals look like without actually seeing them. We're talking about a new kind of symbolism here, the ability to conjure up ideas in our minds without having a specific referent in front of us that we actually see, hear, or smell. We're talking about the ability to live in and embellish a new world of ideas.

But didn't the early humans who lived before this revolution think symbolically? Probably they did, but their capacity for symbolic thought must have been limited largely to verbal or other signs depicting objects existing in the physical world. Some "symbols stand for things that would exist anyhow in the absence of symbolism. . . . We humans, however, construct an amazing repertoire of 'things' that have no existence outside a symbolic context. . . : beings (ghosts, deities), social roles (presidents, bridesmaids), objects (sceptres, stop signs), concepts (sin, authority), acts (baptizing, promising), values (virtuous, chic), and so forth."[2]

It is hard for us to imagine the mindset of people whose symbols don't include abstract ideas. Our imagination boggles at having to imagine people who looked like us but who couldn't imagine. Think of them as being in a hopeless rut, thoughtwise. They had hand axes, and that was good enough for them. If someone died, they left his body behind when they moved on; that was how it had always been. They may have loved their mates and children, and envied others with greater strength or hunting skills, or complained at times, but always in simple, concrete terms, and always within the context of a strong sense of bonding to the village-sized group to which they belonged.

All very well, but how did this new explosion of the mind happen? The most plausible theory I have seen is by Steven Mithen,[3] who draws on both the archeological record and the findings of psychologists who have been examining the development of mental capabilities in modern children. His argument, grossly oversimplified, is that early humans, like very young humans today, developed intelligence in several different areas, independently and along parallel tracks. The language module, a uniquely human evolutionary advance, grew out of a module that regulated individual behavior toward other individuals within the group, the so-called social intelligence module. Another module, natural intelligence, related to the physical environment and concerned skills such as those needed for hunting, gathering, and avoiding predators. A third, technical intelligence, concerned toolmaking and related material aspects of daily life. The independence of these modules from each other allowed them to evolve more rapidly than if they had been lumped together in a kind of general intelligence, but a point was eventually reached where the boundaries that separated them simply broke down—as happens when children reach a certain age.

Mithen's theory may or may not prove accurate, but at least by analogy it can help explain what was going on. When people started thinking across boundaries, between, say, technical and natural intelligence, they were able to devise weapons specifically adapted to different kinds of game, and soon you had a proliferation of specialized tools. When people began to mix social and natural intelligence they were able to imagine animals with human characteristics, as illustrated by the now-famous cave paintings. Rocks and other natural objects could be endowed with human emotions and other capabilities associated with the social environment. These can be seen as the first steps leading to belief in supernatural creatures, occult forces, and many of the religions and superstitions that still populate much of our mental world.

Every chemistry student has seen the experiment in which a solution gradually becomes supersaturated, then suddenly turns into a solid when a single crystal is dropped in. The conditions that brought about the symbolic revolution must have been somewhat analogous. Various attributes of human intelligence, especially regarding language and social competence, were building up gradually, until they reached a critical threshold that produced a breakthrough. Of course the time scale was entirely different, for we measure the symbolic revolution in terms of millennia, not parts of seconds as we do with the supersaturated solution. But when we look at the vast time scales for biological evolution, or even at the five million years it took for anatomically modern people to evolve from our chimplike forebears, the time it took our ancestors to learn to *think* like we do is a mere moment. It marked the beginning of a new form of evolution, the evolution of culture and ideas, that has proceeded ever since at a much faster pace than biological evolution. It was the first big bang of the human mind.

In scientific parlance, our ability to think in abstractions is most probably a by-product of a long period of selection for fitness in specific environments. That by-product had the collateral advantage of greatly increasing our ability to adapt to a wide variety of other environments. This new, uniquely human ability gave the individuals that possessed it an enormous selective advantage when the environment changed, either because the climate changed or because they moved into new environments. Runaway selection followed, and humans that thought as we do rapidly spread into most of the habitable parts of the earth.

The symbolic revolution didn't occur everywhere at once. The archeological evidence is spotty, but suggests it began in East Africa or the Levant, and spread rapidly in all directions.[4] People who thought symbolically simply were better organized than the older populations that didn't. They could adapt more quickly to varied environments and compete more effectively when confronting hostile groups. They were curious, and ambitious, and some of them had the instinct to explore what lay over the next range of hills—an impulse that still impels many modern men and women to regard frontiers as challenges rather than limits.

ENTER RELIGION

One of the more proximate effects of the revolution was the invention of God (or, better, of gods). It seems likely that this invention occurred in many places and took different forms. Or if it started in just one place, it diversified and assumed many forms as it spread out throughout the Old World. Certainly the religious rituals, beliefs, and practices that anthropologists have recorded among huntergatherer societies are very diverse. There are common denominators but one has to dig to find them—like languages.

Perhaps religion started in some places with the attribution of human emotions and capabilities to inanimate objects. When I was in Nepal in the early 1970s I sometimes drove to a holy place called Dakshinkali, at the extreme southwest corner of the valley. Villagers came there from surrounding parts to sacrifice chickens, and an occasional goat, to a local version of the Hindu goddess Kali. A chicken was a significant portion of the total wealth of these very poor people, and I reflected on why they were willing to go to the trouble and expense. I had the impression that the practice had been going on a very long time, certainly for a couple of millennia, perhaps for much longer even than that. I fantasized a bit, and came up with a picture of a Pleistocene hunter who had a narrow escape from a tiger near a peculiarly shaped rock. The story of his escape was retold and passed on from one generation to the next, and gradually it became embellished, the way a good story will. The peculiar rock became endowed with a spirit that played an active role in the miraculous rescue. Eventually people who had been brought up to believe the rock had magic powers started slitting the throats of small birds and animals there, perhaps hoping to fend off tigers themselves, more likely to take out the only insurance available against a variety of misfortunes.

A thousand generations later, people are still slitting the throats of lesser creatures at that rock in the conviction, now hallowed by precedence of unknowable antiquity, that it will do some good, and that no matter what happens, it would have been worse if they hadn't gone to the trouble of making the sacrifice.

Another plausible origin theory is that at least in some places, the spark that brought on religion was lit by schizophrenics.[5] One of my sons, regrettably, suffered from acute schizophrenia and his disjointed ramblings were so transmodular as to be mostly incoherent. But at times he made enough sense to seem to be uttering profundities that gave the impression he was revealing hitherto inaccessible wonders. Some of his peers actually hung on his words and professed to achieve a certain enlightenment from them. My sense is that if he had been born forty or fifty thousand years ago, he might have been worshiped. Unfortunately, he was born too late for that, and a bit too early for the medical breakthroughs now leading to the understanding and possible cure of his condition.

Whatever the precise nature of the spark, one result was an interest in what we now call the supernatural. A schizophrenic shaman may have babbled about a powerful creature half horse and half man, and started a cult of worshipers of a god in this form possessed of powers to make wishes come true. These worshipers might quite naturally come to identify themselves by their "faith" in this particular supernatural entity, and regard all those who did not share this particular suspension of disbelief as outsiders and even as potential enemies. As generations passed, sexual selection probably helped solidify the group's "faith," in that believers of both sexes tended to reject nonbelievers as mates. When conflicts arose with outside groups, a passionate belief in the magical powers of their deity to support them would lend them strength in battle. When they prevailed, oral history would record and embellish their deity's achievement. If they lost, that unfortunate fact would soon be forgotten.

There are, of course, many other theories as to how and when religion started, including the book of Genesis. I favor the ones I have suggested because, unlike Genesis, they don't require the intervention of a deus ex machina. In fact they require no sense of direction or purpose whatsoever, beyond the immediate gratification of currently perceived wants. This is important if you subscribe to the scientific view that evolution is without any specific purpose or aim, but rather follows the short-term, ad hoc process of selection through adaptation to the requirements of the immediate environment.

SOCIAL EVOLUTION BETWEEN THE SYMBOLIC REVOLUTION AND THE NEOLITHIC

In the long run, perhaps the most important single effect of the symbolic revolution was to shatter the old upper limit on how many individuals could cooperate within a group. In earlier times, the effective social unit was limited to an association of kin-based bands totaling a maximum of about 150 individuals. A group that small is relatively egalitarian; you don't need elaborate hierarchies, and there isn't much scope for specialists. Once the symbolic revolution was up and running, however, our ancestors began to expand the level of their social organizations. A profusion of cultural markers became available to supplement genetically based physical recognition as means of identifying members of the in-group. Language, material culture, and religious beliefs could all serve as ways of differentiating one group from another. The ability to think and speak in abstract terms added a new dimension to the way a village-sized group related to its neighbors across the river or on the other side of the mountain. New ways of distinguishing friend from foe opened new possibilities for intergroup alliances, as well as for conflict. Over the course of millennia, group selection by culturally defined societies became increasingly important. The better organized a given group was, the more likely it was to survive challenges both from the environment and from competing human groups. And the successful groups, the survivors, tended to increase in size and complexity as the inevitable consequence of their success.[6]

There were, however, limits on the extent to which societies could expand during the long gestation period that preceded the Neolithic. Limited technology meant limited food supplies and that in turn precluded dense populations except in a very few favored areas. A highly dispersed population was too spread out to permit organization of the large social units that evolved later, after the introduction of agriculture. Given these constraints, which almost always applied at the hunter-gatherer level, the extended tribal confederation represented the most complex society that a population could support. Typically, tribes would have a total population of a few hundred to a few thousand people, divided into several bands speaking the same dialect. Tribal-level institutions would typically maintain peace between bands, provide emergency aid to fellow tribe members, celebrate communal rituals, defend the tribe against predatory raids by neighbor tribes, and authorize the punishment of tribal miscreants. At that level, there would be culturally sanctioned procedures for making decisions, usually on a consensus basis, about war, peace, and major institutional changes.

In other words, during this period our ancestors were able to surpass the limits of reciprocal altruism and work up to the kind of tribal organization that we can still observe in certain parts of the world, or know about from the historical record. I am personally familiar with how tribalism on this scale can work from exposure to it in such far-flung regions as Morocco, Iran, and Nepal. My father's doctoral thesis for Harvard analyzed tribal structures in the Rif mountains of northern Morocco; he recorded his results not only in a technical monograph but in a highly readable novel.[7] Tribalism is still a critically important organizing principle for populations in parts of the Arabian peninsula and the Sahara; in Afghanistan, among the Kurds; in west and central Africa; and in many other places.

This concept of belonging to a tribe is closely related to the largely instinctive urge that leads us to associate most comfortably in village-sized groups. The main difference is that our sense of tribalism doesn't require each of us to know everyone else personally. Symbolic markers can supplement mutual recognition so that we have a sense of community when we meet other members of the tribe, even if we've never met them before. In modern times, this ingrained tribal sense gets diffused and split up between loyalties to several different types of organizations that fill roles in different parts of our personas. Some people, for example, are fiercely loyal to a local football or baseball team, or to a fraternal organization or lodge, or to an employing firm or a labor union. Most of us identify with several different types of groups, and as long as the groups operate in different spheres, feel no conflict between them.

This raises interesting questions: is this propensity to identify with tribal-sized groups instinctive or cultural? Is it part of our genetic inheritance, or is it something we learn during our lifetimes? Were the behavioral changes that occurred during the Upper Paleolithic period purely cultural, or partly cultural and partly genetic? Was there coevolution during this period, as there was in the earlier period that began when our ancestors first became human in a structural, physical sense? Or wasn't there enough time, during the roughly two thousand generations that occurred between about fifty thousand and ten thousand years ago, for natural biological selection operating at the individual level to produce genetic change?

The most reasonable answer is that there may have been some genetic change during the Upper Paleolithic period, but most of it was cultural, or learned.[8] During the early evolution of human behavior, from about 150,000 to about fifty thousand years ago, the balance of the coevolutionary process was different, with genetic change playing a more important role. Then, with the symbolic revolution, the pace of change in human behavior speeded up considerably. Most of the change was cultural, but there was still enough time to allow for some genetic evolution. Finally, during the last ten thousand years, cultural evolution has accelerated enormously, and there simply hasn't been enough time to allow for any appreciable genetic catching up.

This is directly relevant to an understanding of how human societies have evolved, from earliest beginnings to the present and beyond. We still sense different layers of loyalties, starting with the family, moving up the hierarchy to the village, and then ascending a step further to the tribe. The family loyalty is entirely genetic, hard-wired in our human nature. The village loyalty is largely but not entirely so. Tribal loyalties are mostly but not entirely learned. All the higher levels, which we are about to examine, are entirely learned.

Some of these acquired loyalties are mostly primordial, in the sense that we learn them during our infancy, at the same time we are using our innate language ability to learn the specific language of our group.[9] Most of them, however, are acquired at later stages in our lives, and are entirely cultural. I was not born a Red Sox fan, nor was that loyalty instilled in me while I was still learning to talk. I became one while I was quite young, and still am, although I probably would have switched loyalties by now, if my adopted home of Washington, DC, had ever developed a respectable alternative.

Any understanding of human ethical structures as they exist today is bound to be helpfully informed by an awareness of these levels and how deeply they are embedded in our mental machinery.

NOTES

1. Steven Mithen, *The Prehistory of the Mind: A Search for the Origins of Art, Religion, and Science* (London: Thames and Hudson, 1996), esp. pp. 24–30 and chap. 9.

2. Philip G. Chase, "Symbolism as Reference and Symbolism as Culture," in *The Evolution of Culture: An Interdisciplinary View,* ed. Robin Dunbar, Chris Knight, and Camilla Power (New Brunswick, NJ: Rutgers University Press, 1999).

3. Ibid.

4. Jonathan Shaw, "Origins," an interview with Ofer Bar-Yosef, McCurdy Professor of Prehistoric Archeology at Harvard University, *Harvard Magazine* (September–October 2001): 50ff.

5. This idea is not mine alone. See Robert Sapolsky, *The Trouble with Testosterone* (New York: Scribner, 1997). Sapolsky suggests, in the final essay, pp. 243 ff., that mild schizophrenics have provided inspirational leadership as shamans in the remote past—and still do, at times.

6. Carl Coon, *Culture Wars and the Global Village* (Amherst, NY: Prometheus Books, 2000).

7. C. S. Coon, *Tribes of the Rif,* vol. 9, Harvard African Studies (Cambridge, MA: Peabody Museum of Harvard University, 1931). Also *Flesh of the Wild Ox* (New York: William Morrow and Co, 1932).

8. Cf. Peter J. Richerson and Robert Boyd, "Complex Societies: The Evolutionary Origins of a Crude Superorganism," *Human Nature: An Interdisciplinary Biosocial Perspective* 10, no. 3 (1999): 253–89.

9. I shall use the word "primordial" in this context and in this context only in the rest of this book. I recognize that it means different things to different people, and apologize for any confusion, but I know of no other word that comes closer to describing this kind of learning, the kind that occurs so early in life that it can, later on, resemble instinct. Instinct is largely unrecognized, and the individual may control its operation but can never entirely eradicate it. So is primordial learning, though to a lesser extent; it is quite different from learning later in life, which is much more visible, and easier to change.

9.

The Neolithic Period

J ared Diamond's book, *Guns, Germs, and Steel*,[1] describes the transition from foraging societies to farmers and herders in some detail. It was an evolutionary process rather than something that just happened all at once. Many geographic and cultural factors were involved, and it was only possible to move from gathering wild plants to cultivating them, and from hunting animals to herding them, when all of these conditions were favorable. That is, it could only happen when the right plants were growing wild, and/or large mammals suitable for domestication were native. The most favorable circumstances were found in the so-called Fertile Crescent running from the Levant through southeastern Turkey and down the valleys of the Tigris and Euphrates rivers to the Persian Gulf. And that is where the Neolithic first began, about ten or eleven thousand years ago. Later, it began independently in at least five other regions that were similarly favored, although rather less so than the Fertile Crescent.

Another popular book, Brian Fagan's *Floods, Famines, and Emperors*,[2] has a different perspective. Fagan cites climate change as the key factor that triggered the introduction of agriculture. Or rather, climatic factors prevented our ancestors from settling down and growing their food instead of foraging for it until about ten or eleven thousand years ago, when a fairly sudden and drastic global climate shift created conditions under which a sedentary way of life became possible. This shift marked the end of the Pleistocene and the beginning of the present geological era, the Holocene.

Diamond's otherwise excellent explanation may have understated the importance of climate. We now know a great deal about ancient climate shifts, from core samples of glaciers and lake beds and other sources. Throughout the Late Pleistocene era, which covers the period from before the symbolic revolution to the beginning of the Holocene some eleven thousand years ago, abrupt climatic changes were the rule rather than the exception. Tropical as well as higher latitudes were affected by abrupt swings in temperature and rainfall, causing recurrent floods, droughts, windstorms, and the like. By comparison, the climate during the Holocene has been relatively stable. There have been shifts from wet to dry and back, and from colder to hotter, but they have been minor compared to those in the Pleistocene. In my opinion, it is no coincidence that when the weather settled down, so did our ancestors.

Wherever agriculture and animal husbandry replaced foraging, food supplies increased and the population grew. More people meant that when a given space was filled up there would be pressures to expand into neighboring space. If that space was already filled with a hunter-gatherer population, with rare exceptions the farmers would win, because there were more of them. The hunters would either be killed off or assimilated or driven someplace else. Meanwhile the expanding sedentary population, with assured food supplies, could indulge in the luxury of developing an increasingly complex array of specialists, people who ate food produced by others and paid for it by doing other useful things. Pandora's box was opened, and all sorts of unintended consequences flowed that eventually led to writing and what we know as history.

Having said that, are we perhaps overrating the importance of the Neolithic breakthrough, at least in terms of our present analysis? Sedentary agricultural populations leave a lot more traces than a roving tribe of hunters and gatherers. Most archeological "digs" are therefore aimed at investigating ancient city and town

sites, rather than the few scattered traces left by Paleolithic wan-
derers. And quite a few of these digs, these days, are aimed at examining where and when the earliest agricultural populations were
established. We are conditioned by this circumstance to think of the
boundary between the Paleolithic and the Neolithic as a truly critical one, perhaps the most important single leap forward our ancestors ever made in their long trek toward present civilization.

I don't agree, not entirely anyway. In terms of the size of the
"in-group" as perceived by its own members, I see no reason to
believe that the numbers changed much between the Upper Paleolithic and early agricultural settlements. If your kin-based band is
closely associated with other such bands in a tribe of about 150
people, and your tribe is loosely associated with neighboring
tribes in a culture-based confederation of a thousand or so people,
you don't have to change your basic sense of social organization
very much to adapt to a sedentary household inside a village culturally associated with other villages up and down the river.

The features in the archeological record that distinguish the
Neolithic from what preceded it relate to the material business of
earning a living, not to the ethical structures that govern interpersonal relations, including the ethical guidelines that maintain group
equilibrium within the village, and between allied groups of villages.[3]

It may well be that the Neolithic economy spread as rapidly as it
did *because* it didn't require any basic readjustment in the individual's sense of the kinds of groups in which he or she belonged.
We are a pretty adaptable species, but it helps if we can take our
major challenges one at a time. Thus a clam digger on the Baltic
could go on digging clams and keep the same family and clan structures as before, when he started growing a little barley on the side.
Thousands of years later, when the prophet Muhammad introduced
a whole new array of annual ritual events, he grafted them on to
preexisting pagan festivals so the transition to a new ethical system
would be easier. We are a lot more conservative when it comes to
changing our ethics, which are intimately connected to our ideas
about what kinds of groups we belong to, than we are in adapting
to new and better ways of improving our material condition.

I stated in chapter 4 that there have only been three major turning points in the evolution of complex societies: the evolution of people who were physically like us, the evolution of people who think like us, and now. Back during that first hundred thousand years there were most probably a series of important developments that laid the ground for further evolution, but we don't know about them, for it all happened too long ago. Within the last fifty thousand years, however, the record is more extensive. We can now regard the Neolithic breakthrough as a kind of important sub-marker, a set of technological innovations that opened up new possibilities for the development of in-groups based on culture. It did this by creating the preconditions for much greater population density and the evolution of specialists. This led to the eventual replacement of small-scale, egalitarian groups by larger, hierarchically based entities, intensely competing with each other. But that only happened when the land filled up, and whole societies felt pressed to go after each other to obtain scarce resources.

As a very rough approximation, the true Neolithic occupied the first half of the last ten thousand years. It ended earlier in regions where it first started, and persisted longer in regions remote from those centers. Some feminists maintain that it was a period during which females ruled and the world was at peace.[4] This is certainly an inaccurate picture. There is abundant archeological evidence that there were many minor wars during that period.[5] Nevertheless, societies were more egalitarian and there was less intergroup conflict than in the tumultuous period that followed. The prevailing ethical system was that of the village, based on reciprocal altruism, more instinctive than learned, clearcut in its sense of correct versus incorrect behavior, largely self-enforcing. The relations between groups of villages involved a newer layer of unwritten rules, but over the preceding forty thousand years they had been worked out in tribal form to a degree that ensured a fairly high level of predictability and hence comfort. The Neolithic was, in terms of the evolution of complex societies and the ethical problems they represented, the calm before the storm.

NOTES

1. Jared Diamond, *Guns, Germs, and Steel: The Fates of Human Societies* (New York: W. W. Norton, 1997).

2. Brian Fagan, *Floods, Famines, and Emperors: El Niño and the Fate of Civilizations* (New York: Basic Books, 1999).

3. Please note, however, that now that we have actual villages on the ground, and part of the archeological record, we can start using the term "village" literally rather than metaphorically. As I specified on page 56, for earlier periods I was using the word "village" to refer to groups of upward of 150 people united by reciprocal altruism, even though the group at that time consisted of migratory foragers.

4. Riane Eisler, *The Chalice and the Blade* (San Francisco: Harper, 1988).

5. For one example, see Carl Coon, *Culture Wars and the Global Village* (Amherst, NY: Prometheus Books, 2000), pp. 89–91.

10.

The Golden Age of Culture

During the Neolithic, social cohesion was maintained through a fairly balanced mixture of innate and learned ethical principles. Kin-based ties and reciprocal altruism still played a major role in the management of the largest social groups that were extant at the time, so the need for complex, learned rules of behavior was relatively limited. But the basis for these more complex rules was already in place. One of the key elements was religion, which could provide a sense of community to fellow believers that transcended the inherent size limits of the village. Another was language, including dialect, which extended the physical recognition factor by informing individuals as to whether the stranger was truly an outsider or was at least distantly related. We should include nonverbal patterns of communication in this category. A third element included those physical qualities that were easily recognizable: racial types, or how people looked, and visible elements of the material culture, like how people dressed. All these elements were able to give the individual a sense of how, if at all, he or she related to that stranger in the marketplace. They provided shades of gray to supplement the older, more primitive sense of community based on facial recognition.

The distinguishing feature of the epoch that followed the Neolithic was a considerable expansion of all three of these elements in both scope and complexity. The result was the emergence of coherent social groups much larger than anything our species had achieved before. Individuals identified themselves as members of such groups by some mixture of the three elements we have just identified: religion, language, and appearance. The proportions of these elements varied, but they were all, except for race, based on mental constructs. Because of this both the groups themselves and the factors that held them together could evolve quite rapidly.

What I am describing is, of course, the efflorescence of what we sometimes call culture.[1] The introduction of culture as the organizing principle for large social groups was highly successful in an evolutionary sense; it was the dominant template for almost all human societies for millennia, and still is, in many parts of the world.

The cultural template allowed the size of the in-group to expand almost indefinitely, subject only to physical limits on available food supplies, and competition with other cultures. Ethical guidelines evolved that were clear and enforceable, so that within these enlarged social units, most people would not only not cheat, but would condemn cheating wherever it happened, and take actions to apprehend and punish cheaters in their society, even at some cost to themselves. Respect for authority developed that was strong enough to predispose individuals to pay taxes and accept whatever other burdens their position in society implied. Individual authority figures, including kings, warriors, and priests, came to adhere to prescribed ways of behaving toward each other and toward those of inferior status. All these rules were backed up by a strong sense of what was right and what was wrong.

This massive breakthrough on the cultural front paved the way for most of the kinds of developments over the last five or six millennia that students study in their ancient and medieval history lessons. It allowed for hitherto inconceivable degrees of specialization, making possible the construction of pyramids and ziggurats and the like, as well as extensive irrigation works and other, less benevolent innovations like tax collectors and armies.

HOW CULTURE-BASED SOCIETIES GOT STARTED

Once Neolithic groups were able to merge in ways that allowed large numbers of individuals to cooperate for mutual benefit, the payoff was enormous. But how did people get there in the first place? Let's not forget that we have renounced teleological explanations for these matters. We cannot assume that our remote ancestors developed larger and more complex societies because they were guided by some vision of the payoff that would accrue generations after they died. They did what they did for more proximate reasons; the end result was essentially circumstantial rather than intentional.

Usually, a tribe or a small coalition of villages would either absorb or be absorbed by some of its neighbors. Separate village-level identities would continue, but would be subordinated within a larger, culturally distinct society. As that new society grew, and developed ways of maintaining solidarity, it might absorb neighboring groups that had not yet reached its level of social complexity. It was an evolutionary process that developed irresistible momentum as it went along.

But we need to know how the process started in the first place. In all probability, one of the early points of origin—perhaps the earliest—was the Fertile Crescent, and we shall take that as our example. In that favored region, something along the lines of the following scenario probably occurred: Increased population densities eventually led to new kinds of problems, like how to apportion scarce water for irrigation, or how to resolve recurrent conflict between neighboring groups. As long as people were thinly scattered, population pressures could usually be handled by migration. If a village or a tribe happened to occupy land near a river flowing through a desert, and the river level fell due to drought, they could move or spread out, and still survive. But if there were settlers all along the river, all more or less equally dependent on it for irrigation, the same drought could bring catastrophic pressures. Hungry villagers couldn't just wander a few miles upstream or downstream without intruding on someone else's territory, nor could they head off into the desert with any hope of feeding themselves. They had no place to go.

Eventually, something had to give. Either the population in these areas went up in good times and got cut back in bad ones, or people had to devise new ways of coping. Every other animal on the planet has followed the first course, but in a few places, a few of our ancestors chose to innovate, using their uniquely human capacity for imagining concepts and organizations that had never before existed. They created new institutions that could maintain order and discipline within much larger groups of people than before. This gave people new ways of coping with environmental disaster. For example, granaries could be constructed to store excess food in good years to be consumed in lean ones. This required a new class of authority figures at the top, new rules with bureaucrats to implement them, and warriors to defend the realm against outsiders and to enforce discipline inside it. Kings, bureaucrats, and warriors soon discovered the utility of enlisting a professional hierarchy of priests to help ensure the stability of their rule. Enter a brand-new chapter in the history of human social evolution. Village and tribal structures continued, but a new class of kings, warriors, and priests arose that ruled over realms that could be an order of magnitude larger than anything seen before.

There are other scenarios, other possible reasons for the creation of culture-based societies out of formerly independent smaller entities. Trade, for instance. Or warfare between tribes, in which the winner either absorbed or annihilated the loser, in either case imposing its rule on the latter's territory. Probably all of the above, and more, occurred during a bygone era for which we have little hard information. The salient points for this study are, first, that the transition did happen, and second, that we can plausibly construct reasons why it happened naturally, not through the intervention of a supreme being that inspired certain leaders to shepherd their followers out of the wilderness.

CULTURE AND GROUP SELECTION

Empty space is a great peacemaker, while crowding breeds conflict. So it was probably inevitable that the increasing population pressure on the land that took place during the Neolithic would lead to an increase in the frequency and intensity of conflict between groups. True, conflict between families, or between village-level groups, was reduced when some higher authority was established that could knock heads together and keep the peace. But that didn't end conflict, it simply escalated it to a higher level. As the Neolithic progressed, to be succeeded by more complex culture-based societies, village- and tribal-level squabbles evolved into wars between larger and larger groups.

Internal cohesion soon became the ticket to survival in a Hobbesian, dog-eat-dog contest between different groups, each animated by a more or less powerful sense of cultural identity. I belabored this point at some length in my book *Culture Wars and the Global Village*, and will not repeat all the arguments here. Suffice it to say that the fierce loyalties one sees nowadays that animate groups in places like the Balkans and the Middle East, and that led to so much conflict between them, are the end result of a long period of essentially Darwinian evolution, in which the groups that could command the total loyalty of their members tended to win out over those which didn't.[2]

This pattern of internal cohesion and external conflict became so widespread that it can fairly be compared to the warp and woof of a gigantic textile, a vast tapestry on which was woven the multicolored history of our ancestors. That long and complicated saga has been marked by nearly continuous conflict, much cruelty both within cultures and between them, and a great deal that is even now seen as noble and inspiring. It was also marked by an explosion of technology, much of it initially inspired by arms races, that led to increased understanding of the natural environment, and increasingly sophisticated means to turn nature's bounty to human advantage.

CONCERNING KINGS, WARRIORS, AND PRIESTS

The typical social organization we are describing in this chapter was hierarchical and authoritarian. At the top was a ruling caste of nobles headed by a king, who specialized in telling the rest of the nation what to do, and in managing relations with other nations, frequently punctuated by wars. I am, of course, oversimplifying, but this was the basic pattern for Bronze and Iron Age "civilizations" around the Mediterranean, in Mesoamerica, in South Asia, in China, and indeed in every area when a relatively easygoing Neolithic society made the transition to a more complex social level.

There are good reasons why the transition was to authoritarianism rather than to a more democratic form of society. There was no universal code of ethics that applied equally to commoners and nobles. Relations within the village continued to be managed fairly well in the old ways, and the village ethic could be adapted to a community of overlords who among themselves constituted a village-sized community. But there was nothing in the prior experience of the species to bridge the gap between commoner and overlord. Perforce, the overlords relied heavily on new symbols of authority, backed by instruments of coercion, to maintain the integrity of the whole kingdom (or land, or whatever the society called itself).

Every kingdom developed its own kinds of pomp and ceremony. The king couldn't know everyone in his kingdom, at least to recognize, but every king worth his salt made sure they all knew him. Palaces and pyramids and all the other appurtenances of royalty that we still encounter in many parts of the world can be seen as devices to ensure that everybody knew who was in charge. And the ruling class had the weapons and the physical power to back up its authority. But there was another ingredient in play that smoothed over the rough edges of the new situation by providing an ethical system that usually made coercion unnecessary. That was religion. Over and over again, the masters of the new societies formed an alliance with the priests. It was a singularly potent form of symbiosis. The overlords protected and pampered the priests, who in turn kept the peasants in line. It's a sweetheart arrangement which has persisted till modern times and still can be detected even in some of the most modern nation-states.

One further feature needs to be noted—the hereditary principle. The new kingdoms may or may not have inherited rules of succession from the villages and tribes that preceded them, but their rulers almost always insisted on being succeeded by their offspring. There are serious drawbacks to that arrangement, because there is no way of assuring that the son will have the qualities that made the father successful as king, baron, or whatever. But any other way of passing on the various attributes of power is uncertain and can lead to internal conflict, unless pretty firm rules of succession are in place. Early in the golden age of culture, those rules were not in place. And once hereditary succession was firmly entrenched, it appealed to the "selfish genes" of the people in power. If an urge to pass on your power to your offspring is as much innate as culturally determined, that could explain why it lasted so long—and why it still happens from time to time—as with the late dictators of Syria and North Korea, who maneuvered to install sons as their successors.

It's time now to take a closer look at this phenomenon of religion. We first observed it in the Upper Paleolithic, as part of the symbolic revolution. But religion didn't take off and show its full capabilities until the golden age of culture.

RELIGION

Think of a modern concrete building complex, or a large interstate highway junction. It isn't just the concrete that holds everything together. There are steel rods buried inside the concrete that provide the inner strength that keeps everything from collapsing under stress.

Religion plays a similar role in societies that have evolved beyond the village stage, into the relatively large and complex groups we're considering in this chapter. There's a lot more at work here than what you see. You can see people observing public ritual events, which contribute to a general sense of group solidarity. You are less likely to observe them in their private prayers, which also contribute to the sense of belonging to the group, while meeting deep personal needs. Least visible of all are the ethical do's and don'ts that govern the ways individuals of various occupations and classes act towards each other. But religious beliefs permeate these ethical constructs. They not only inform people as to what is acceptable behavior and what isn't, they also contain their own system of rewards and punishments, which usually relate to the fate of the spirit after the body dies. Children learn all these matters as integral parts of their early religious instruction, which illustrates them through parables and sacred texts.

It is instructive to reflect on the changes that took place in the ethical structures children learned, after the golden age of culture had taken root. In Neolithic times, the village child must have absorbed religious instructions telling it how to behave during ritual events, often tied to the agricultural cycle, and how to manage interpersonal relations within the village. But most of the latter instructions were based foursquare on reciprocal altruism and went back to a much earlier era: love thy neighbor, don't steal, covet not thy neighbor's wife, and so forth. They were culturally imposed embellishments on instinctive behavior patterns that were already there, and were correspondingly easy to assimilate. By contrast, the poor child in the cultural era had to learn a lot of new precepts that were not innate at all: accept your station in life, be good and you'll go to heaven, women are inferior, and so forth. There were many more embellishments, bells and whistles as it were, for such children, and to make the situation even more complicated, there had to be two sets of instructions, one for nobles and one for commoners. So those steel rods that held the society together were under a lot more stress than they had been in earlier and simpler times.

Religious doctrine and the institutions that managed it reacted to this increased stress by becoming much more elaborate and demanding. The priesthood expanded in size and authority. It usually developed along hierarchical lines, with some popelike figure (or figures) at the top who often assumed the role of a direct communications link with the deity (or one of the deities). Ethical do's and dont's became more specific and detailed. Meanwhile, secular instruments of coercion that backed up religious doctrine and ecclesiastical authority grew stronger as well.

CONCLUSION

The golden age of culture represented the first full flowering of a uniquely human genius for symbolic thought. That capacity held the potential for social cooperation on a much grander scale than before, but for a long time after it was first employed—upward of fifty thousand years—its potential was only tapped in a few limited ways. A loose association of village-level societies was about the limit, until a combination of pressures combined to burst the dam of conservative thinking and unleash the enormous potential of much larger cooperating groups. The critical threshold was the evolution of mechanisms to ensure group solidarity based almost entirely on symbolism. It was symbolism, running all the way from the pomp and ceremony associated with royalty, to the early, mind-numbing training of the peasant, that gave every member of the group a solid sense of where he or she fitted into it, and an enduring loyalty to its support and preservation.

The forms this new plant took as it emerged from the soil of the Neolithic included arms races and advancing technology, hierarchical political structures, and increasingly elaborate and doctrinaire religious beliefs and institutions. All these and more combined synergistically to unleash an explosion in human creativity. Our modern elites can look back on this period with some disdain, for it was punctuated by frequent wars, and there was precious little democracy about it, or respect for human rights. Feminists can regard the scene with particular dismay, for the emphasis on fighting involved a corresponding derogation in women's rights, leading to circumstances women today are only gradually overcoming. The Founding Fathers of the United States were tapping into a deep vein of history when they spoke out against tyranny.

But when all is said and done, the epoch was a glorious one, marked by episodes of nobility and brilliance as well as by degradation and oppression. We can safely conclude, as we look back on this huge and rich saga, that we'd never have gotten as far as we have today, if we hadn't gone through it. In particular, it forced our ancestors to explore new ground in developing ethical structures to cope with totally new ways of organizing societies. The architecture of ethics, formerly a kind of ranch house, developed a second story. Recently, our immediate ancestors erected a third. We can see outlines of a fourth. I see no reason why our more distant descendants shouldn't reach for the stars, or at least the other planets, and eventually erect a fifth. As long as we use our capacity to imagine, the sky's the limit.

NOTES

1. The word "culture" has many meanings. I use this definition, from *The New Heritage Dictionary*, 2d College ed., s.v.: "culture: . . . the totality of socially transmitted behavior patterns, arts, beliefs, institutions, and all other products of human work and thought characteristic of a community or of a population."

2. This view is challenged by those anthropologists and other social scientists who still cling to the increasingly outmoded belief that group selection isn't possible, as all selection takes place on the individual level. I hope I disposed of this argument in chapter 5. Group selection between culturally identified units has been taking place for a long time and continues to pop up in various places right up to the present. All you have to do is read the daily newspapers for proof.

11.

Fast-Forward
to the Nation-State

We take for granted the fact that the world's population these days is organized into nation-states, but we don't always recognize that this is a relatively recent phenomenon. In terms of the time frames we've been using, the nation-state system as we now know it was born yesterday. Many historians believe the system began in 1648 with the Treaty of Westphalia, but it took a while before its implications became evident. For example, until a mere couple of centuries ago, most of humanity was organized politically the old-fashioned way, with hereditary aristocracies in charge. Nevertheless, profound changes were taking place in the seventeenth and eighteenth centuries, as technological progress produced a strong middle class, and as scientific advances led to a more sophisticated understanding of our place in the cosmos. Change continued with a vengeance in the nineteenth century, and its pace is still accelerating. At first there were only a few states that mattered, but when the colonial powers withdrew the number climbed rapidly. Now there are 191 recognized states with votes in the UN General Assembly.

Every state represented in the UN today owes its existence to a unique set of circumstances. It is impossible to generalize about them in a way that covers them all, but in very broad-brush terms, here are some markers that can help define the new order and differentiate it from the one it supplanted:

- there is now a new (or perhaps very old) sense of egalitarianism;
- there's a fixation on inviolable and precisely marked national boundaries;
- religious codes have been subordinated to national secular legal systems; and
- there is a widespread effort, not always successful, to subordinate ethnic loyalties to a newer sense of national patriotism.

THE DECLINE OR FALL OF HEREDITARY ARISTOCRACIES

Until quite recently (in terms of the time frames we have been using), the world was the dominion of kings and emperors, assisted by the other aristocrats who surrounded them and ruled over subsidiary fiefdoms. There were, of course, exceptions, including a few upstart colonials in places like New England, and a larger number of people in parts of Africa and elsewhere who were still organized at the tribal or village level. But the general pattern of a hereditary monarch who surrounded himself with hereditary nobles was the norm. It was a way of life sanctified by the blood of two hundred generations of men who had died upholding its values.

Some monarchies still survive, though usually the sovereign's personal authority is much less than it used to be. Morocco is an example of one of the few survivors where the king actually wields power. The late king, Hassan II, survived a tumultuous period in his country's history because he was an exceptionally astute and adroit politician. It remains to be seen whether his heir will retain control, will gradually relinquish it and become a monarch in name only, or whether the throne itself will pass into history.

Nepal is another apparent exception. It was strictly a feudal society, living in near-total isolation until after the Second World War; and while the will to change into a modern state is now evident, the experience is still insufficient. Meanwhile, the monarchy survives because it is needed as a unifying symbol. I am fond of Nepal and its people, but I also find it interesting as a kind of refuge area in which one can still observe traces of how the old system used to work. For example, the Nepali language is the lingua franca of the country, but it has a version designed for the royal court that is so different as to constitute a separate language. Hierarchical distinctions are ubiquitous and essential. It is impossible to talk to someone else without using subtle indicators as to whether the person you are addressing is superior, inferior, or of equal status. Many of the old court languages developed this way, throughout the world.

Here is another example of the then-prevailing mindset: I sometimes played bridge with a Rana general, one of the last of the feudal overlords who ran the kingdom of Nepal until after the Second World War. He loved to give parties and set a lavish buffet for his guests. When his guests finished the course, they were expected to set their plates down under the buffet table, where they would be concealed by the wide tablecloths hanging down on either side. Servants would crawl along from the kitchen under the row of tables, pick up the used plates, and pack them off without their presence intruding itself on the honored guests. The procedure seemed ludicrous to me, as an American, but was perfectly consistent with the prevailing social attitudes of that particular class of aristocrats, and indeed with many other such groups.

There is no clear pattern to the ways that the hereditary monarchies fell. England muddled through a series of events that eventually reduced its monarchy to figurehead status. France was less patient, and erupted in a bloody revolution. Principalities in central Europe coalesced along linguistic lines and then, a generation or so later, abolished or neutralized their aristocratic leaders. In Russia, the czar and his nobles fell late, and hard. The Ottoman Empire tottered along until the end of the First World War, then collapsed into a motley collection of new states; most of them became republics. China decisively repudiated its imperial tradition. In India the British Raj tolerated the princes and let some of them go on running their fiefdoms for a while, but when the Raj pulled out in 1947, the new Indian government cut them off at the knees.

I know of no theory that can predict what kind of society will emerge when a traditional, hereditary system collapses. Every country follows its own track. Out of the ashes of the old kingdoms and empires all sorts of countries have arisen: democracies and military dictatorships and communist workers' paradises and even a theocracy or two. The salient point for present purposes is that the old hereditary class structure that dominated for so long is gone, except for a few areas where it is hanging on by a whisker. And it went pretty suddenly, in terms of the time frames we have been using. If we are looking for important milestones, that one stands out.

Perhaps the machine gun, as much as anything else, marked the transition from the golden age of culture to its successor, the age of the nation-state. Its widespead use in the First World War finished off the traditional employment of massed infantry in fighting land wars, and that change contributed more than is generally recognized to the European aristocracy's loss of power. Renoir's classic film *Grand Illusion*, has the following evocative dialogue between two officers, one each in the German and French armies, both aristocrats, about the real losers in that global conflict between armies formed from citizens rather than mercenaries.

de Boeldieu: Neither you nor I can stop the march of time.

von Rauffenstein: I don't know who will win this war, but whatever the outcome, it will mean the end of the Rauffensteins and the Boeldieus.

de Boeldieu: We're no longer needed.

von Rauffenstein: Isn't that a pity.

de Boeldieu: Perhaps.[1]

What caused this rather abrupt demise of a social pattern that had remained in the ascendancy almost everywhere for five thousand years? A simple answer is that it broke down because life got too complicated. The hereditary basis for selecting leaders is guaranteed to produce a fairly high percentage of failures and near failures. It is satisfactory only when stability is more important than the ability to adapt to changing circumstances. Circumstances changed slowly during most of the golden age of culture, but toward the end the rate of change accelerated rapidly. Technological advance and the accelerating proliferation of specialists, plus an enormous expansion of trade and commerce, led to the emergence of a middle class with enough knowledge to oppose the old system, and, eventually, enough clout to get rid of it.

The old system held on as long as it did because people are more conservative when changing basic values—including concepts of class status—than in adapting to new technology. The nation-state was the logical outgrowth of increased trade, improved technology, and increased understanding, but it took generations after the pressures generated by these factors built up before they could burst through the conservative wall protecting attitudes toward class structure.

Religion played a complex role during the transition to nation-states. Schismatic movements sometimes supported change, but not the mainstream elements of the old religions. In Europe, the bishops supported the old order as long as they could, and then, when the aristocracy collapsed, adapted as best they could to the new circumstances. Some faiths and denominations adapted more readily than others, but for the most part the priesthoods of our time are still hierarchical, still doctrinaire, and still conservative in the values they instill in the children of their followers. They tend to coexist in an uneasy equilibrium with a state system that presides over "citizens" who may follow several divergent faiths. The principle of the separation of church and state, while far from universal, is nevertheless honored in one form or another in most of the modern state systems at this time.

THE NATION-STATE AND THE PRINCIPLE OF TERRITORIALITY

The idea of defining countries in terms of fixed territorial boundaries has not always been in vogue to the extent that it is today. In ancient times, when clusters of population were widely separated, a tribe might have had a pretty clear sense of its own territory, and might have recognized that some other tribe on the other side of the mountain had turf of its own, but there would be a considerable space in between that belonged to neither. It's analogous to a group of islands in the Pacific, each with its own territory, separated by the sea. This was the case until quite recently with many of the Bedouin tribes in the Sahara.

In the eighteenth and nineteenth centuries, the Sultan of Morocco ruled over those tribes in the adjacent parts of the desert which formally acknowledged his sovereignty. Nobody took the trouble to delineate the exact territorial extent of his domain, and it wouldn't have been much use even if they had. The sultanate's power and reach varied; tribal sheiks were more likely to make the pilgrimage to the capital and kiss the hem of the sultan's robe if the sultan was a strong one; and anyway, the tribes not only moved around, they often shifted their loyalties as well. So Morocco, as a country, never had permanently fixed and delineated boundaries along its Saharan frontier until the French and Spanish moved in and drew lines on the map.

The issue came to a head in the 1970s when Spain vacated the Spanish Sahara and Morocco claimed it on the basis of historic tribal affiliations. Many people didn't understand Morocco's claim, or were unwilling to accept it, since it involved an old-fashioned and unfamiliar concept of sovereignty. I became personally involved, as the US State Department's Country Director for North African Affairs, in arguments with the department's lawyers and with representatives of the department's African Bureau, which manages our affairs with countries south of the Sahara.

The lawyers, and much of the American press, saw the former Spanish Sahara as an entity with defined boundaries, usually colored yellow on the world's map, and assumed it should be treated as a separate political entity undergoing decolonization. It seemed logical to them that the new regime should be formed by the indigenous inhabitants, represented by the Polisario.* Morocco, accord-

---

*"Polisario" is a Spanish acronym for "Frente Popular para la Liberacion de Saguia el Hamra y Rio de Oro," or "Popular Front for the liberation of Saguia el Hamra and Rio de Oro." Saguia el Hamra and Rio de Oro were two provinces administered by Spain which combined when the Spanish withdrew to become what is now known as the Western Sahara. The Polisario movement was created from desert tribes of the region, and originally opposed the Spanish. However, when the Spanish

ing to that line of thinking, had no more status than any other neighboring state. This infuriated the Moroccans, who felt that since the territory had always, more or less, belonged to it in the past, its recently changed status should be seen as the last phase of a decolonization process for the whole country that had begun in 1956. This almost theological issue has never been resolved to everyone's satisfaction, and the "issue of the Western Sahara" is still one that concerns the peacemakers in the UN and elsewhere.

The African Bureau, meanwhile, was horrified at the prospect of a nearby territorial dispute being resolved on the basis of tribal history. After all, almost every so-called nation in Africa south of the Sahara exists within boundaries that were drawn by the former colonial powers, and most of them cut across tribal and cultural lines. My colleagues in the African Bureau didn't even want to think about changing established international boundaries for any reason whatsoever, since they were convinced that any such action could destabilize the whole region. This fear still characterizes mainstream thinking for the United States and other status quo powers, though it has been weakened a bit by the Yugoslav breakup and other such developments.

Like many other large mammals, our species has an innate instinct for territoriality. Adult males mark their turf and then fight to defend it. But the conflict over the western Sahara suggests that the territorial instinct can take shape in different ways. The Moroccan position, based on tradition, was and remains weak and even suspect in the eyes of many Western authorities. The more modern view regards states as inviolable, and considers all but the most minor border adjustments as unacceptable. It is as though the state were an individual, and loss of any significant piece of its sharply defined territory equated to the loss of a limb. Unprovoked military aggression across a recognized international frontier was a casus belli for the US government in Korea in the early 1950s and again, in Kuwait, in the early 1990s.

---

withdrew and Morocco moved in to assert its control, the Polisario emerged as a national liberation front fighting against Morocco for independence. They have survived to this day only because they have been given sanctuary and other forms of support in neighboring Algeria.

As long as societies were divided on cultural lines, precise boundaries were less important as elements of group identity than the cultures themselves. A dynasty based mainly on the cultural homogeneity of its subjects could lose territory and recover quite nicely later on. But when nation-states took over, culture lost much of its force as the final determinant of group identity. Some of the new states were mostly homogeneous, but others were not. New ways of assuring group identity were needed. Flags, national anthems, and pledges of allegiance came into their own as symbolic reinforcers of the new, enlarged sense of national identity. But that sense also required a more tangible definition of the state. Precise boundaries on the ground thus came to replace precise cultural markers as a basis for group identification.

THE ELEVATION OF SECULAR LAW

For purposes of this analysis, the law can be defined as an explicit and detailed codification of behavioral rules that coexists with and supplements a society's ethical do's and don'ts. The child absorbs a general respect for the law at an early stage in its development, but learns the details later on.

We don't have much hard information about the origins of legal systems. We infer that before the invention of writing, attempts to codify rules and behavior usually involved a priestly caste. Until the modern nation-state era, the law has been intertwined with religion to some degree or other. Hammurabi's Code in Babylon, the earliest written legal code we know, is essentially secular but begins and ends with a prayer. In the Middle Ages, the "umma" or Islamic world based its law on the Shari'a, a legal system developed out of the Koran by Islamic scholars in the first several centuries of the Muslim era. In other lands and at other times, relations between the law and the prevailing religion took many different forms. While there were occasional tussles between religious authorities and secular ones, with varied outcomes, for the most part the law and the clergy maintained a mutually supportive relationship.

Some Islamic states still base their legal systems on the Shari'a, or have reintroduced it after a period of secularization. This, however, is viewed by most other observers as regressive, and that in itself is a litmus test of the benchmark this chapter describes. Most of the more modern nation-states draw a sharp distinction between secular and religious law, and insist that when the two doctrines conflict, the secular law takes precedence. This reflects a sense that the law of the land has replaced religious instruction as the steel frame holding society together, and that culture-based loyalties must, therefore, bow to the interests of national unity.

I would argue that for a modern nation-state to become fully functional, it must establish its secular law as taking precedence over whatever forms of religious law are still observed within those religious or ethnic communities that maintain a separate identity within the larger community. The state can provide exceptions, as in the case of granting tax exemptions to established religious denominations. But if the state is to survive, or at least not slide into dysfunctionality, then ultimately the law of the land must predominate.

Much the same principle applies to conflicts that arise between loyalties to ethnic communities within the state, and the state itself. We shall be looking at the general problems posed by this kind of conflict later on, but meanwhile we need to look at the specific problem of ethnicity, which has to be defined as something different from culture, if we are to achieve any clarity in this whole analysis.

FROM CULTURE TO ETHNICITY AND BACK

One authority, anthropologist David Eller,[2] describes two schools of thought about ethnicity. According to one school, "ethnicity" is something the individual assumes, something ascribed, like kinship; its "givens are inexpressible, inexplicable, overpowering, and coercive." To me that sounds like a sense of cultural identity learned primordially, along with the native language and the ethical instruction that goes with it. Eller then cites another school of thought which holds ethnicity is primarily self-defined, that is, when individuals in a group *feel* they are united by ethnic ties, that's all the proof that is required. In fact the ties may be based on lineage/race/ bloodlines, or on a quite different mix of some or any of the foregoing plus religion, language, manners and customs, geography, history, and so forth.

Eller argues that when one group collides with another, its leaders will exploit distinctive features of the group's culture to affirm their agenda while reinforcing group solidarity. Such leaders will be selective in invoking the past and may even create mythical parts of their collective history to help mobilize their peers for present purposes. Thus conflict between ethnic groups is not about culture, no matter what the antagonists may say. It is about other issues, which vary greatly, with cultural arguments used as ". . . a justification . . . the basis of entitlement of the group to certain other stakes and rights. . . ."

This helps us avoid the current confusion, so evident in today's press, regarding the use of the term "ethnic."[3] Ethnicity can now be seen as an aberrant, metastasized form of culture. It's kind of a sex-crazed expression of group identity, where adrenalin and testosterone take over from the cerebral cortex. It normally happens only when cultures collide, and it gears the group up for conflict much the way glandular changes in the individual prepare him for hand-to-hand combat.

This distinction between a primordial sense of cultural identity, and circumstantial ethnicity, is useful when we interpret the history and even prehistory of our ancestors. I would postulate that over and over again, cultures have collided and become inflamed into ethnic hatreds. But then, after the shouting and fighting was over, people settled down and reverted to culture in its primordial sense.

I would also postulate that one of the distinguishing features of the modern state system is the uncommon frequency with which dormant cultures have erupted into belligerent ethnicities. It is like a global epidemic; new ones are springing up a lot faster than old ones are dying down. The problem of ethnic divisions within the state system has reached the point that in some regions, it now threatens the basic assumptions on which that system rests.

FROM SUPERSTITION TO SCIENCE

From the dawn of the symbolic breakthrough and perhaps earlier, people have been watching the sun and the moon and the stars. Not knowing any better, they naturally assumed the earth stood at the center of the universe. As religions evolved, they drew on the fact that these celestial objects were known to everyone, but remained unreachable and mysterious. Divine attributes were assigned, and experts sprang up who foretold the future from the myriad possible conjunctions of the stars. Every culture developed origin myths, fables explained to the very young that gave them the best explanation of life that they could muster, and one that reinforced the ethical bonds that kept them together. The great monotheistic religions worked out a cosmic topology that seemed eminently plausible under the circumstances, with heaven up in the celestial firmament, and hell down underground.

A few early Greek sages, among others, developed more sophisticated ideas, but this simplistic view of an earth-centric world was shared almost universally until Copernicus and Galileo introduced modern astronomy. Their ideas were resisted, especially by the religious authorities, who as usual were conservative guardians of the status quo. But from then on, astrologers lost much of their power, while humankind as a whole gained in wisdom as it came to appreciate its diminished role in the overall scheme of the cosmos.

A second revolution in our thinking came with Darwin, who offered a convincing explanation of how a sentient human being could have evolved through entirely natural processes, without divine intervention. This was an even tougher pill for the ecclesiastical authorities, since it made it unnecessary to posit the existence of a soul, or some human essence that would live on after death. If first you remove the prospect of heaven and hell, and then raise questions whether there is life after death, much of the coercive force of the world's great religions goes by the boards.

There are many other landmarks in humanity's struggle for enlightenment during this long period of aristocratic rule and ecclesiastical domination. I shall not describe the entire evolution of scientific discovery and thought, as any reasonably competent analysis would require an excursion far beyond the purview of this book. Suffice it to say that the transformation of our social attitudes that ushered in the nation-state was intimately connected with the rapid evolution of science that occurred during the same period. It is safe to say that neither could have occurred without the other.

A DIFFERENT PERSPECTIVE

Describing the contemporary nation-state system, in a single chapter of a book this size, is like describing an elephant in three or four brush strokes. You have to leave almost everything out, including much that is central to any serious attempt to achieve even a modest level of understanding. And yet, a Thurber or a Hirschfeld could actually communicate quite a lot in three or four brush strokes, perhaps even the idea of an elephant. The trick is to pick certain features of that elephant and concentrate on conveying their essence, while leaving everything else out. It's a bit like standing a great distance away from the subject, when you can see only a few salient features of the outline. And that is precisely the approach I took in the earlier chapters on social change during our prehistory. But that was relatively easy, because our collective knowledge of what went on during those many millennia that preceded the advent of writing is pretty sparse—and it gets even sparser the farther back we go.

Let's go back for a moment to the Middle/Upper Paleolithic transition, that first big bang of the human mind that I described in chapter 6, when the symbolic revolution was occurring. Our genetically transmitted social skills may have sharpened a bit since then, but our ancestors were, as best we can tell, essentially the same kind of people we are. If so, we can perhaps look for parallels between the issues they faced, and the world we see around us today.

They faced a world in which a whole new concept of togetherness or social bonding was opening up. They had to accept, as members of their own peer group, individuals that they didn't recognize, who were not part of the group they had grown up with. They had to learn to recognize a whole new array of symbols as means of identifying them, and distinguishing them from total strangers or foes. And then they had to develop and internalize a whole new set of rules as to how to behave toward them.

We cannot tell what the intermediate stages of this period of rapid change were, not exactly anyway. From our distant vantage point the transition was fast, almost sudden, but even so it probably took centuries even where it first started, and then it took tens of millennia to radiate out to other parts of the inhabited world. If we had eyewitness accounts from that period we would doubtless find that there were many fits and starts, steps forward and steps backward, as our forebears painfully and tentatively inched their way into a new social order. In their way, they probably argued as much about the right way to proceed as we are doing now. There was probably as much indecision and anguish as today.

In this context, we can regard the present nation-state era as a transitional period, and a relatively fleeting one at that. It is but a stepping stone from an ethic based on culture to an ethic which embraces a global community. The key factor is a new ability to think in terms of an in-group that embraces diverse ethnic and religious communities. Since we have succeeded in achieving relatively harmonious in-groups of this nature in some parts of the world, some of us, at least, have broken the old mold. The seed has been planted, and while it may take many generations before it embraces everyone, it is probably unstoppable—just as the new era of symbolic thinking was, about fifty thousand years ago.[4]

NOTES

1. The dialogue is in French, but I have taken the translation provided in the English subtitles. The film was produced in 1938. Eric von Stroheim played von Rauffenstein, Pierre Fresnay played de Boeldieu.

2. David Eller, *From Culture to Ethnicity to Conflict* (Ann Arbor: University of Michigan Press, 1999). I have drawn on his concepts, while assigning a different and relatively unfamiliar meaning to the term "ethnicity."

3. The original meaning of "ethnic" related to race, but that association has been lost in current usage. Now the term has been debased in current journalese to mean almost any kind of group identification that exists parallel to and below the state level.

4. It could be stopped if some catastrophe eliminated much of the world's present population, reducing the rest to isolated pockets. The least unlikely such catastrophe would be a major nuclear war, which seems unlikely now that the cold war has wound down. An epidemic of a new and incurable disease seems even less likely given our advancing technology. A collision with a large asteroid is a statistically insignificant third possibility.

12.

The Present Transition
(The Second Big Bang)

This chapter zeroes in on an era of about two centuries, the twentieth and the twenty-first. It's been a busy period, so far, and promises to get even busier. A conceptual earthquake is rearranging basic attributes of our societal framework—how we fight, how we coexist with the environment, even how we think. Any one of these seismic changes would constitute a major milestone in the overview we've taken of human social evolution. Together, they portend the most sweeping change in the human condition that has occurred since that big bang of the human mind that happened about fifty thousand years ago.

Consider that for almost all of the long history and prehistory of our species, we have been taking whatever we could from the planetary environment, as though its resources were inexhaustible. During the past few generations we have run out of space, we are now running short of water, and we are discovering that even the air around us is a finite resource.

Meanwhile, our mastery over the environment has increased. During the last several generations the amount of raw energy available has increased enormously, the frictional cost of trade and transport has plummeted, and food supplies have become abundant even as population has mushroomed. Right now we are going through a cybernetic revolution that is multiplying many times over our ability to acquire and use information of all kinds.

Finally, consider that for at least the last ten thousand years a prime shaker and mover in the grand drama of the social evolution of our species has been conflict between groups. Consider further that while much of that conflict has taken peaceful forms, the ultimate arbiter has always been recourse to war. Then reflect on our present condition, where a major nuclear war is no longer an option—unless we want to risk destroying civilization as we know it, and rendering much of the planet uninhabitable.

THE LINGERING PROBLEM OF A MAJOR WAR

We managed to survive the cold war without a major and catastrophic exchange of nuclear weapons, but we are still a long way from abolishing war in general. The world still has to worry about outright war between India and Pakistan (which could turn nuclear), troubles centered on North Korea, Israel versus its neighbors, and many other conflicts that exist at least partly at the state level. The United Nations works at keeping the peace, and it has some successes to show for its efforts, but conflicts involving powerful states are still beyond its practical reach.

Despite these threats to world peace and stability, the world's nation-states still haven't given up any appreciable amount of sovereignty where issues of war and peace are involved. The UN Security Council has acquired some moral force, but moral force doesn't cut much ice when a nation believes its vital interests are involved. President George W. Bush's war on Iraq has shown the world all too clearly that the UN Security Council can keep the peace only when its efforts are strongly supported by at least some major powers, and are opposed only by minor players.

Meanwhile, nation-states in adversarial positions continue to play the same old game of power politics, and when they approach a conflict situation they often play that supremely dangerous game of chicken. The world continues to sit on the edge of a kind of volcano, looking down into a potential maelstrom of nuclear horror. And it isn't getting any better: with the growing threat of international terrorism the situation is actually getting worse.

ETHNIC CONFLICTS, WEAPONS OF MASS DESTRUCTION, AND TERRORISM

The world was less comfortable during the cold war, when we faced the constant possibility of nuclear holocaust, but it was a lot tidier. When the cat goes away, the mice will play. That's approximately what happened when the Iron Curtain crumbled. A lot of conflicts between states and within states popped up when it was no longer a major interest, bordering often on the vital, of one or the other superpower to keep the lid on. Local wars, insurrections, coups, rebellions, irredentist movements, and other disorders increased, and upset the existing order in countries all over the world. The nation-state system was challenged regionally, by assaults on the sanctity of recognized governments and national borders, and systemically, by global trends that seemed beyond any one country's control.

These disturbances are not dying down. If anything they seem to be popping up ever more frequently. There is no status quo ante in our future. What, if any, are the trends?

Nuclear Weapons

Nuclear weapons have been humanity's number one nightmare ever since Hiroshima. The prospect of having them freely available to a couple of hundred different states, all independent, many competing with their neighbors and sometimes coming into conflict, is a prospect that has galvanized responsible statesmen everywhere. In this field as in no other, almost everybody recognizes the need for effective international control mechanisms. Many of the world's most talented statesmen, international lawyers, and diplomats have devoted their lives to keeping the nuclear genie bottled up.

It has not been an easy task. For a while, the cost and complexity of nuclear weapons put them beyond the reach of most states. But as nuclear technology became cheaper and better known, and as more states crawled out from under the influence of the superpowers, the line became harder to hold. By the turn of the century, the nonproliferation effort resembled a foundering boat, springing leaks all over the place.

Genocide

Genocide, now commonly referred to as "ethnic cleansing," is an extreme form of conflict. It is usually based on ethnic rivalries, in which a stronger group attempts to eliminate a weaker group and take over its land. The aggressor normally uses some combination of mass killings and terror tactics aimed at forcing the surviving losers to flee. The practice has been around for a long time, but in the past, outsiders tended to see it as a regional matter; powerful states that didn't have much equity in the action generally limited their interventions to charitable contributions for the needy and pious expressions of concern. Only recently have all the leading nations, under the aegis of the United Nations, agreed that genocide anywhere is a crime against humanity everywhere, and deserves to be treated as such.

It is instructive to look at this issue in terms of the evolution of international legal institutions over the last century, and where they appear to be heading. The International Court of Justice, established after the First World War, set up regular procedures for handling disputes between sovereign states. The Nuremburg trials, after the Second World War, established the principle that individual leaders of a nation that surrendered unconditionally after a major war could be hauled into court for their crimes. More recently, ad hoc international tribunals have been established to try individual leaders responsible for several recent tragic events of a genocidal nature. These include the wars that followed the breakup of the former Yugoslavia, the massacres in Rwanda, the Serbian attacks on the Albanian inhabitants of Kosovo, and the killings in East Timor. The growing need for this kind of international tribunal led to the establishment in July 2002 of the International Criminal Court. That body ". . . can bring charges of genocide, crimes against humanity, and war crimes against individuals as long as they are a national of a state that has ratified the treaty, or the crime was committed on the territory of such a state, or the Security Council refers a specific case to the court."[1] A majority of states belonging to the UN have joined. The major holdout, so far, is the United States.

All these steps have accompanied and been helped by a considerable expansion in international law. The lawyers and the peacekeepers have worked hard over the last few decades, both to define what constitutes "crimes against humanity" and to develop institutional mechanisms to punish the people who perpetrate them. They still have a way to go, however, before the rules are defined sharply enough, and enforcement mechanisms have grown strong enough, to constitute an effective response to genocide anywhere in the world.

Terrorism

Terrorism is a separate but overlapping problem. Its roots are ethnic more often than not. When a group that has major grievances senses that it isn't achieving what it would consider justice by discussion or negotiation, pressures build up. Terrorist cells start forming when at least some members begin to sense that the group as a whole is heading for extinction, or some other fate that is almost equally unacceptable. There is thus an important distinction between the terrorist and the ordinary criminal. The criminal is behaving for selfish reasons, but the terrorist fights for the survival of his group.

It follows that ridding the world of terrorism requires a somewhat different approach to the one national law-enforcement authorities follow in dealing with criminals. Standard police techniques can be useful, and should be coordinated as effectively as possible across national frontiers, but that isn't enough. Peacemakers with authority have to get to the group which is spawning the terrorists, and deal with its problems.

This all sounds obvious, but unfortunately, the authorities in most of the afflicted areas have insisted on labeling all terrorists as criminals, and most of the rest of us have supinely accepted their terminology. We shall have to get over that myopia if we are ever to get going on solutions as opposed to temporary patchwork. And clearly, those solutions have to be global. National solutions are no longer an answer. This will be particularly true if our worst fears are realized and serious terrorism goes nuclear.

Some solutions may require adjustment of national boundaries. Fortunately the old reverence for the sanctity of these lines someone drew on a map generations ago has become somewhat diluted. Experience has shown that boundaries can be changed without catastrophic repercussions. Now the peacemakers need to be a bit bolder in pushing the idea of boundary adjustments. Sometimes a little tinkering is all it takes to transform a flaming ethnic quarrel into another example of diverse cultures coexisting peacefully.

THE CONTINUING AMORALITY
OF INTERSTATE BEHAVIOR

Meanwhile there is work to be done on the level of interstate relations. In the middle of the last century, when I was beginning my diplomatic career, we were not encouraged to think beyond the narrow confines of the national interest. The morality of statecraft was based on Machiavelli, not the Golden Rule. The prevailing ethic was that ". . . there are national interests consisting mainly in security, political independence, and well-being of the population . . . that . . . have no intrinsic moral quality, and cannot be subjected to moral scrutiny or judgment."[2]

International law regulated some aspects of interstate behavior, but it was a dry and strictly utilitarian codification, precise in its application, leaving everything that was not explicitly regulated to the states. The nation-states, often impelled by cold war pressures, continued to use a wide array of "dirty tricks," including bribery, disinformation, and various other forms of covert actions, up to and including torture and political assassinations. World opinion has gradually turned against such forms of covert manipulation, particularly the more egregious varieties, but there is still no clear and accepted ethical principle that they are all more or less bad. And yet, if you apply the Golden Rule to relations between states, all these dirty tricks are bad in that they involve lying or cheating or some form of outright violence against other members of the society.

Eventually, future generations will be brought up to believe that the same ethical guidelines people use in dealing with people around them should also govern the conduct of interstate relations. Don't cheat, don't rob, don't lie, and so forth. Those decencies translate fairly readily into rules like these:

- Economic and technical assistance programs that reflect the donor's political as well as purely developmental objectives, but no covert funding.
- Strong overt information programs, but no disinformation or "black propaganda."
- No "surgical strikes" or other military or paramilitary operations in unfriendly territory, except by the UN itself.
- Diplomacy through traditional means; no kidnappings, hijackings, or assassinations.
- No more covert operations, except as sanctioned by the UN against rogue states.
- Megacorporations should stop bribing officials of corrupt governments, with opprobrium falling equally on each party.

This new application of old rules can eventually achieve a stature great enough to discourage transgressions in all but the most extreme conflict situations, and such transgressions will in themselves often constitute grounds for exercise of the UN's coercive authority.

ECONOMIC GLOBALIZATION

For the economists and other architects of economic development, globalization is essentially an extension of the older idea of free trade. By freeing up the movement of goods and capital across national frontiers, the strongest producers have flourished and the total amount of goods and services available in the world as a whole has been increasing even faster than the global population. The movement toward integration is being led by the World Trade Organization (WTO), which has developed enormous clout in recent years, even as it has aroused enormous public opposition. There are several reasons for this opposition, based on differing and even conflicting concerns.[3] They illustrate that there are ethical as well as practical difficulties that beset the road we all have to travel if we are to achieve a more integrated and harmonious world community.

1. *The first concern* is that the WTO gives excessively high priority to the interests of big business, especially the multinationals, and the finance ministries of the more powerful states. Other important concerns, notably for the environment and for human rights, are downgraded. This concern may have been exaggerated in some circles but there is ample evidence that it is well founded.

2. *The second concern* is that the WTO erodes national sovereignty. Everyone recognizes that these days, if a country wants to prosper economically it has to join the club, and giving up a piece of its sovereignty is part of the price. But not everyone agrees the price is worth paying.

3. *The third concern* is that the WTO is democratic only in theory; in practice, the big states and multinationals do as they will, and the rest fall in line. This concern is clearly justified. On the other hand, it's probably the only way the WTO could have succeeded. The important issue is where the WTO goes from here, not how it got here.

4. *The fourth concern* is that the WTO makes the rich richer and the poor poorer. This is a complicated issue. Both the rich countries and rich individuals have gotten richer faster than the rest of the pack. The evidence for the impact of economic globalization on the very poor is contradictory and unclear.

Everybody wants to become more prosperous, and so does every nation, but pursuit of economic objectives frequently comes crosswise with other concerns. Most states recognize they'll have to compromise their sovereign rights a bit on matters of trade, but how about their sovereign right to govern their people as they see fit, when it comes to a question of human rights? And how about their right to manage their domestic economies, when that collides with global environmental concerns? There are a tremendous number of issues here, and most of them are exceedingly complex. The diplomats and international legal experts have their hands full. They are working out a lot of detailed procedures governing interstate relations on specific issues, but present opposition to the WTO shows that there is a felt need for something more than a jungle of new technical workarounds. There's a vacancy here, a gap waiting to be filled. What can we do to ensure that the collective good of our entire species takes precedence over the interests of smaller groups? And what mechanisms do we need by way of enforcement? The need is for a forum where an international consensus can be forged, backed by global institutions capable of translating that consensus into effective action.

POPULATION, REFUGEES, AND MIGRATION

There is little point in a rerun here of all the familiar arguments about the population explosion and what it's causing in terms of human misery and environmental degradation. Anyone likely to read this book is already conversant with at least the broad lines of the situation. The populations in the rich countries have more or less stabilized, while those in most of the poorest countries have not. Many countries are somewhere in between, struggling to lower their birth rates, with varying degrees of success. The key is not coercion but improvements in the economic and social status of women. Ethnic and other regional conflicts are making a complex situation worse; millions of desperately poor people have been turfed off their natal places. Most of them, and millions more, are trying to migrate to places where they can at least hope for a decent life.

Concern about the population explosion has been growing for at least the last fifty years. By now population stabilization is a central objective of many national and international economic development programs. It is a hot ticket item on the agendas of many UN subcommittees, while a veritable army of Non-Governmental Organizations (NGO's) lobby in the rich countries and maintain programs in the poorer ones. Refugee and migration problems engage the attention of the top officials of the United Nations, as well as leaders of most of the world's nation-states. They have come to occupy a distinguished place among the world's major migraines.

Some people are coming around to the view that a strong supranational authority is needed. It is needed to ensure that effective family planning and health services are available on the ground in all countries. It is needed to stand down one of the world's great religious faiths which has blocked family planning programs in major parts of the world. It is needed to secure enough resources from the wealthier countries to pay for the care and feeding of refugees, and build permanent solutions to their problems. And it is needed to lead world opinion in forging a new global ethic about the value of an individual human life and the responsibility of the rich toward their poorer brethren.

THE ENVIRONMENT

Who owns the earth? When a necessary resource is freely available, the supply has to be unlimited or eventually the number of people using it grows to the point that there isn't enough to go around. Once it becomes a scarce commodity, people have to change their attitudes, and perhaps even their way of life. That's what happened along the banks of the Tigris and the Euphrates ten thousand years ago, when periodic water shortages forced our ancestors to enter the Neolithic, with all the wrenching social adjustments that implied. And it's what is happening right now, as we come up against the finite limits of the atmosphere and the world's water supply and a host of other planetary resources.

For a hundred thousand years we were part of the biosphere. For the last ten thousand we've been exploiting it. Now we have to start managing it. Some of the adjustments that are being forced on us can be made on the national level, and in the more successful state systems this has begun to happen. But climate and the weather don't respect national boundaries. It's now obvious that environmental concerns that involve the earth's atmosphere and oceans cannot be handled piecemeal on a national basis. They can only be managed through global cooperation. We need more international treaties, more supranational mechanisms to enforce them, and eventually, we need to construct ethical standards as to how we share these finite and increasingly valuable natural resources that we all used to take for granted.

THE NEED FOR GLOBAL GOVERNANCE

It's like a confluence of big rivers, merging into one mighty stream. We need effective international control of weapons of mass destruction, particularly the nuclear ones. We need international authorities that can keep interstate and interethnic disputes from erupting into outright war, and adjudicate and enforce measures to punish acts of genocide. Most of us see a need for a global regulatory framework for the multinationals, that can control their more anti-social and anti-environmental proclivities. We need stronger international mechanisms to manage and control the worldwide refugee and migration problems. Some environmental problems can only be resolved through a global approach.

Perhaps one or two of these urgent needs might be met by treaties between existing states, that commit them to cooperation in specified areas. But that's essentially what we have now, and it isn't enough. No, seen in the context of the whole long history of the social evolution of our species, the long-term answer to these current problems has to be some kind of a central global authority that can bring together conflicting views and produce a consensus; that can coordinate; and that can, when push comes to shove, coerce. The present nation-states must gradually give up significant bits of their sovereignty as this evolution proceeds, much as the thirteen states had to give up some of their individual rights as the price for joining the United States. The long-term goal has to be a strengthened UN, or some successor organization, that has its own military force and the power to raise revenues directly, rather than depending on contributions from member nations.

The only alternative may be a descent into international anarchy with catastrophic results for humanity as a whole, and perhaps even for all life on our planet. One lesson that emerges from earlier sections of this book is that our species is in the middle of a violent transition and simply does not have the option of stopping the process, or even slowing it down appreciably. We are all like the man in a barrel going over Niagara Falls. It is too late for us to change our minds. But let's not allow that analogy to confuse the fact that we are dealing with a much longer time frame. Social evolution proceeds much faster these days than it did during, say, the Neolithic, but we still measure steps in generational terms and major change still takes centuries. If we can achieve the goal of an effective world government in another century or so, that will probably be good enough. Meanwhile the task is not only to build for the future but to survive.

Setting our course for the next couple of decades is a different matter from determining our long-term goals. One of the current masters of the art of realpolitik, Zbigniew Brzezinski, has just produced a book that suggests practical steps to get us past the more proximate global problems we have been examining.[4] He takes the international political scene as it exists today, with all its motes and blemishes, and sketches a practical sequence of necessary changes that will eventually lead to a durable global order. He posits that the United States is uniquely positioned to move this process along, starting with forging stronger transatlantic ties with an expanding Europe, and moving on to incorporate additional power centers into what will gradually take over as a zone of law and stability that encompasses everyone. I am reminded of the old Moroccan distinction between the "Bled al-Makhzen" and the "Bled as-Sibaa." The former was the "Zone of Government," meaning those parts of Morocco where the sultan's rule was observed and people paid taxes, while the latter (which my late father translated as the "Zone of Insolence") was those outlying regions where the leaders might recognize the sultan as their nominal leader, but woe betide any tax collector who ventured onto their turf. Brzezinski's vision, for me, implies a gradual process during the coming century in which a global Bled al-Makhzen gradually, and for the most part peacefully, absorbs the outlying regions and brings them within the ambit of a world order in which disputes everywhere are resolved peacefully, and global challenges are addressed by everyone collectively.

Brzezinski does not pay much attention to the UN in his analysis. My own sense is that the UN has a central role to play in the process, even in the early stages. UN peacekeeping forces are already contributing to the resolution of, or at least control of, troublesome disputes in many regions. I believe the time is ripe for the establishment of a standing UN military force designed to control local conflicts that don't involve important interests of the major powers. The Security Council would, of course, control the use of such a force. I also believe the time is coming soon when global agreement may be possible on some kind of a UN tax, perhaps starting with a minute tariff on international financial transactions.

When the UN has an armed force of its own and an independent source of revenue, it will for the first time begin to resemble the kind of global governing authority the world as a whole needs. It will take a long time to develop its potential, but our species will have crossed a critical threshold. The high road toward one planet, one people will lie open before us.

NOTES

1. Peter Singer, *One World: The Ethics of Globalization* (New Haven, CT: Yale University Press, 2002), p. 118.

2. Robert Toscano, "The Ethics of Modern Diplomacy," in *Ethics and International Affairs: Extent and Limits*, ed. Jean-Marc Coicaud and Daniel Warner (New York: United Nations University Press, 2001). The quote, from page 45, is Toscano's paraphrase of Kennan's dictum as expressed in "Morality and Foreign Policy," an article in *Foreign Affairs* 64, no. 2 (Winter 1985/86).

3. I have summarized the four concerns from chapter 3 of Singer, *One World*.

4. Zbigniew Brzezinski, *The Choice: Global Domination or Global Leadership* (New York: Basic Books, 2004).

13.

America at the Crossroads

As the new millennium began, the United States had at least a theoretical choice between continuing a general policy of leadership through cooperation, and leadership through domination. As the world's surviving superpower, with a military budget roughly equal to those of every other nation combined, the United States could, perhaps, dream of imposing its vision of the future unilaterally, over a diverse and contentious gaggle of nation-states. But few observers ever thought the United States would actually try to pursue such a dream—until the new Republican administration took over the country in January 2001.

George W. Bush won the election of 2000 through a series of technicalities, not through a majority vote. Before the election, the campaign rhetoric was confined primarily to domestic issues. It was only after the Republicans had squeaked through to their narrow victory that the public became aware that a radical new foreign policy was taking shape. The so-called neoconservatives, based mostly in the Pentagon, were for the most part contemptuous of the UN, considering it an obstacle to the advancement of US interests, rather than a body through which those interests could be promoted. They appeared convinced that America's superior military strength not only made an assertive, unilateralist stance toward the rest of the world possible, but also made such a stance morally imperative.

On one issue after another, the new administration's positions reversed those long advocated by previous administrations. Both the decisions themselves, and the manner in which they were conveyed, reflected a deep-seated distrust of the United Nations, and a determination to resist any infringement, however small, on US sovereignty.

NUCLEAR NONPROLIFERATION AND THE ABM ISSUE

In the early 1980s President Ronald Reagan upset a lot of observers by announcing his "Star Wars" initiative, an ambitious effort to develop missiles that could intercept incoming ICBMs. Experts pointed out that this project would cost a fortune and still might not work; and that to the extent it did work it would violate the Anti-Ballistic Missile Treaty with the USSR and be destabilizing. But the Reaganauts never got close to achieving a capability to deploy a national ABM system, so the issue of violating the ABM Treaty remained moot. Furthermore, the Soviet Union was imploding and the strategic threat the United States faced was changing as well. With terrorism on the rise, and nuclear technology increasingly widespread, the chances of a nuclear attack via ICBM was fading, while the possibility of a nuclear weapon delivered by other means was increasing.

In 2001, the new Bush administration revived Reagan's Star Wars initiative and plunged ahead with the necessary funding. It didn't make much sense to many observers, since the administration's announced purpose was no longer to defend against an increasingly improbable threat from the other nuclear superpower. Its stated aim was, rather, to prevent "rogue states" from engaging in nuclear blackmail against America and its allies. No one in the administration could explain why such a rogue state, if it did develop a nuclear capability, would choose to commit suicide by launching an ICBM attack on the United States. And even if it was willing to risk sudden national extinction, why wouldn't it choose some other less costly and overt means of delivery? Never mind, the government's public relations staff moved into high gear and so did the program itself. Most of the rest of the world protested, including the Russians, our contractual partners in the ABM Treaty. Nevertheless, in December 2001 President Bush announced that the United States was exercising its right of withdrawal under the terms of that treaty and giving the requisite six months' notice.

The Russians eventually acquiesced in the United States withdrawal, but the abrupt way the administration handled it didn't go down well in most countries. Our allies drew the implication that the United States was more concerned with defending itself in some future nuclear crisis than it was in protecting them. Another implication was that the United States wanted a free hand in developing a space-age nuclear capability, which could eventually enhance its offensive as well as defensive capability. All in all, the affair struck much of the rest of the world as indicating an ominous shift away from consultation toward unilateralism on an issue—nuclear weapons and the strategic balance—that vitally affected everyone.

GENOCIDE AND THE ICC

During the Clinton administration, the United States participated actively in the extensive negotiations that led up to the 1998 Rome Statute creating the International Criminal Court (ICC). The central issue was whether and to what extent the court would have the power to act independently, without the approval of UN member states. The United States position, mindful of the concerns of conservative members of Congress, was that ICC actions should require prior approval of the Security Council, which would give the United States a veto. Most of the other parties objected, fearing this would leave the new body toothless and ineffective. Various compromises were devised which gave the United States substantial guarantees that the court would never act capriciously or vindictively against United States citizens or interests. In late December 2000, one of the Clinton administration's last acts was to sign the treaty establishing the new body. This was only a first step, as the United States would have to ratify the treaty before committing itself to its provisions. Clinton's stated purpose in signing was to let the United States remain a party to more negotiations that would further define the authority and limits of the new court in ways that would meet remaining US concerns.

The Rome Statute entered into force on July 1, 2002, after the required number of states had ratified it. But meanwhile, in May 2002, the Bush administration declared the earlier United States signature null, withdrew from all participation in the ongoing preparations, and began a public campaign opposing the treaty. The official line has been that while the United States cannot stop almost all the rest of the world from supporting the ICC, it can and will insist that all United States personnel everywhere should be outside the court's reach. This stance deeply disappointed and angered our traditional friends and allies, and put us inside the same tent as Libya, Yemen, China, and the recently expired regime in Iraq.

We are confronted with a paradox. What, one might ask, are the leaders of the most powerful country in the world afraid will happen, if the United States joins the ICC? Are they likely to be hauled to the court at the Hague for war crimes? Are they contemplating the commission of such crimes? Both questions are absurd. The United States has the clout to see that ICC activities will not be directed against it, or its citizens, and it will retain that clout for the foreseeable future. The administration's stance seems grounded not on reasonable fears for its citizens, but on the desire to accommodate certain domestic groups, and their congressional representatives, whose worldview is dominated by a suspicion of "foreigners" that approaches paranoia.

THE ENVIRONMENT AND THE KYOTO PROTOCOL

Global warming, with its potentially catastrophic consequences, has been a subject of hot debate for decades. Almost everyone agrees it is happening, and a strong majority of qualified scientists believe that human activity is a major contributor to the trend. In 1997, some 170 nations, including the United States, signed the Kyoto Protocol. Thirty-nine industrialized nations agreed to reduce or limit their greenhouse gas emissions by 2012. Although the protocol left many details to be worked out, including future participation by India and China, it constituted a serious first step toward securing global recognition of the problem and establishing some form of coordinated global action.

In March 2001, President Bush summarily announced that the United States was withdrawing from the whole excercise. Europe, Japan, Canada, Russia, Australia, and most other nations decided to go ahead without the United States, and many of Kyoto's shortcomings were resolved in conferences in July and November 2001. US nonparticipation remains an important issue between the United States and most of the rest of the world.[1]

POPULATION AND FAMILY PLANNING: THE "GAG RULE"

One of the first steps President Bush took after his inauguration was to reinstate the so-called gag rule. It was first imposed under President Reagan, and revoked by Clinton. It forbids use of United States government funds[2] to support nongovernmental foreign agencies, if their operations outside the United States involve provision of abortion services, including counseling or referrals on abortion, or if those agencies lobby to make or keep abortion legal in the countries in which they operate. It applies even if the agency supplies abortion-related services only with non–US Government funds. If, for example, a British family-planning organization's India branch even mentions the abortion option, even though abortion is legal there, it is not eligible for any US AIDs funds. The gag rule is only applicable outside the United States because it would unconstitutionally infringe upon freedom of speech if it were applied domestically.

This is not an issue that grabs headlines, like global warming or the ABM question. Nevertheless, the arrogance and intrusiveness of this gag rule has done a great deal to convince an army of dedicated welfare workers and others throughout the world that the Bush administration is out of touch with contemporary realities and, far from being an ally, constitutes a major item in the list of the world's current problems. The issue is a particularly sensitive one for those concerned with women's health and reproductive rights.

AND FINALLY, THE INVASION OF IRAQ

In February and March of 2003, the world stood at attention while the United States geared up to invade Iraq. President Bush's spokesmen initially claimed Iraq had supported the Taliban and the 9/11 attacks, but the United States was unable to substantiate this. Then came the explanation that Iraq was developing weapons of mass destruction that endangered world peace. A coalition led by France insisted that the UN inspection teams be given more time to substantiate this charge. But by then the United States and a "coalition of the willing" that included Britain and several other countries, with massive armed forces in place, was poised to attack. With military facts on the ground increasingly dominating the political argument, the question became not whether to attack, but whether a political compromise could be worked out at the UN that would provide the Security Council's approval.The showdown came when the United States and its allies withdrew a compromise resolution that France had promised to veto, and attacked Iraq without UN sanction.

President Bush correctly regarded the issue as a test of the future relevancy of the United Nations Security Council (UNSC). But in a peculiar inversion of logic, he seemed to think that if the UNSC failed to support his military gamble in Iraq, on his terms, and he went ahead anyway, the resulting loss of the UN's credibility should be blamed not on his action, but on those who opposed it.

Bush threw down a gauntlet when he opted for war without UNSC approval. He said, in effect: "Follow me or be damned. If the rest of you fellows want the UN to be relevant, stop opposing me." He believed he had a mandate to clean up a disturbed part of the world, but his source of authority was little more than the fact of his nation's military superiority. He wanted a consensus of other nations to sup-port him, but he didn't express that desire with any particular conviction; and he may simply have been reflecting the public opinion polls that showed most Americans considered international support important. Coming on the heels of other decisions like those described above, it looked to a lot of Americans, and to most foreigners, as though a new Roman emperor was striding on to the world stage, announcing the advent of a global Pax Americana.

A year after US military forces took Baghdad, victory remained elusive. Guerrilla activity showed no sign of dying down. If anything, it was on the upswing, including in the sensitive, Shia-dominated south. There were no weapons of mass destruction. The Bush administration was forced to turn to the United Nations for help in arranging a transition to a new Iraqi government. The professed American role as liberator was tarnished by exposure of inhumane treatment of Iraqi prisoners.

All in all, this adventure in American triumphalism has produced little but one disaster after another. Although Bush's spokespersons continue to try to put the best face they can on the fiasco, the administration has lost credibility almost everywhere. The election in November 2004 will show whether the American public has finally come to understand that military superiority alone will not solve American's problems.

ANALYSIS: WHY THE BUSH ADMINISTRATION HAS BEEN BEHAVING THIS WAY.

George W. Bush and his closest advisers have been totally dedicated to winning the election in 2004. They have shown a fervor and dedication that surpasses normal political ambition. To this end, the president has been handing out favors to core elements of his natural constituency, favors that he and the recipients both know would not be available under a Democratic administration. The gag rule, a crude intervention into foreign family-planning operations, curries favor with his conservative Christian backers. Those voters most offended by it probably would not vote for Bush anyway. Repudiating the Kyoto Protocol gratifies certain big business interests, notably in the fossil fuel industry, helping to ensure big financial contributions for the next election campaign. The ABM program guarantees long-term contracts for the defense industry. Repudiating the International Criminal Court plays on latent xenophobia among his constituents and supports the worldview of his so-called neoconservative advisers.

The neoconservative worldview evolved during the last fifteen years or so among a group of American intellectuals who identified American interests closely with those of Israel's Likud Party. The distaste for and even contempt of the United Nations that the neoconservatives displayed can be explained partly as a reaction to Israel's many years of isolation in the UN. I do not want to overstress this theme, however, as there are other roots to the neoconservative penchant for unilateralist policies. Its main strength as far as the president is concerned is that so far, it has sat well with many American voters who normally are only minimally politicized. The swagger, the confident brashness, the "my way or the highway" stance seem to have brought him a high level of public approval. He was helped by the 9/11 terrorist attack in New York City, which allowed him to play on the fear of a shocked public.

In chapter 5, I discussed the conflicting impulses of egoism and altruism that motivate individuals within a socially united group. I identified them as ". . . the two poles between which all our human urges and constraints play their roles. They are the goalposts that define the playing field, the yin and yang of human nature." If one expands the scale to the level of interstate relations, with the nations of the world as the individual players, then the neoconservative influence on our foreign policy has dictated that United States behavior in the international sphere has recently been almost entirely egoistic.

It is true that the State Department, the foreign community, and the internationalist and progressive elements of the United States public still argue for a foreign policy of persuasion, not coercion. Ever since the president was inaugurated, these forces have been waging an intense struggle for his support. So far they have won some battles, but the record suggests that they have lost many of the more important ones. The rest of the world sees America in a new light. For the first time, respect is tinged with fear.

FURTHER ANALYSIS: WILL UNILATERALISM WORK?

Our chimpanzee and gorilla cousins manage their small social units fairly well on the principle of unilateralism. The biggest and most powerful male is the boss, and rules as long as no other male comes along that can beat him. Our earliest human ancestors worked out a different way of achieving social equilbrium within the group, based on mixing a sense of altruism with raw egoism. This allowed individual members to cooperate without reference to a pecking order based mainly on brawn. It was a successful formula, but for most of human history as well as prehistory it applied only to individuals within the group. As far as outsiders were concerned, might was right, at least in the final analysis, when problems between groups escalated and conflict became unavoidable. Empires arose when there was one winner and several losers. The former king became an emperor when he whipped all the other kings in the neighborhood and reduced them to vassals. The empire would last a generation or two, then wither away to be replaced either by a change of management or a complete rearrangement. Life went on and societies continued to grow larger and more complicated. It was evolution within whatever outer limit then prevailed for the maximum size of the in-group, the social unit within which people had learned to cooperate.

American military dominance is so great at this moment in history that it is conceivable that the American gorilla could impose a kind of Pax Americana on most of the rest of the world. There are many practical reasons why this would be very difficult to achieve, and why any apparent success would soon prove ephemeral. But there is a broader principle at work here, which would foredoom any such effort to early failure.

We need to look again at the Hobbesian principle that dictates that while in-groups may achieve internal cooperation, they are fated in the long run to fight each other. Our study suggests that this principle breaks down during those unusual periods when new factors allow the maximum size of the coherent social unit to leap upward. At such times a basic confusion of ethical standards prevails for a while, until the larger social units establish themselves. The individual whose primary loyalty was to a traditional social unit is faced with a need to transfer it to a new and larger one. When such an individual manages this shift, hitherto unforeseeable vistas open up for advancement and achievement. A world that had seemed to be disintegrating gradually transforms itself into something much better than anything that went before. A Neolithic clam digger on the Baltic whose parents and grandparents had all died within ten miles of where they were born might travel to distant shores and join the retinue of a lord. A talented Armenian in Aleppo might migrate to Hollywood and become a film producer.

The Bush administration, according to this logic, is dysfunctional because, on the world stage, our president is acting like an alpha male gorilla when he should be leading the way into a new synthesis. The aggregate of nation-states which he is trying to dominate is no longer a jungle in which the members vie for power and battle it out when they cannot reconcile their differences peacefully. There are so many powerful factors impelling the comity of nations toward ever greater cooperation that the old system of might makes right simply does not work any more. The ancient Golden Rule of common human decencies has to be introduced and accepted as the foundation of a new order governing state relations on a global scale. There's no turning back. The evolution of human societies is taking another turn on the ratchet. George W. Bush's nostalgic assumption that he can play Caesar is a dangerous illusion.

THE LONG AND THE SHORT OF IT

The next few years are critical. If the neoconservative unilateralists remain in power in Washington, and continue on their present course, they will make the United States a militant, autocratic travesty of its former self, while the rest of the world trembles in its shadow and begins to unite and rally against it. Within at most a generation a world united in opposition to American hegemony will find ways to break it. The comity of nations will resume its search for effective global governance. The grand march of human social evolution will continue. But where the United States could have been the unquestioned leader in that quest, it will have been reduced to a bit player.

There is no possibility that America's present military superiority can last. It isn't just a question of how much money the United States Congress is willing to appropriate. As long as other countries feel threatened by American military superiority, they will try to catch up in any way they can—by developing their own advanced weapons technology, by forming regional anti-American alliances, and even, in some cases, by supporting terrorist groups. It may take a decade or two, but Pax Americana cannot long endure if it is built on the kind of imperialistic policies of the early years of the Bush administration.

There is a better path for the United States, and it doesn't require its leaders to become pacifists. If the Bush administration had fully supported the International Criminal Court, it could have led an international campaign to have Saddam Hussein indicted for crimes against humanity. The charges would have been more than justified, and would have resonated across the world. Eventually, an international military force, under the UN flag, could be in Baghdad, introducing a new and more humane regime, and bringing Saddam and his principal co-criminals to justice.

The United States can lead by persuasion and diplomacy, backed up by military force under UN auspices. The neoconservative alternative of posturing and threats, backed up by the unilateral exercise of force, leaves the UN twisting in the wind, fighting for its survival in a world that needs it ever more urgently.

JUST WARS VERSUS UNJUST WARS

A new ethical principle is coming into focus. In general, it reflects the growing realization that the world needs a global authority that can act decisively to achieve solutions to global problems. In particular, it reflects the diplomatic crisis in New York that preceded the United States attack on Iraq. That principle can be summed up quite simply: wars between nations are presumed to be illegal and ethically wrong unless one of the parties is operating under some kind of United Nations mandate, in which case the action is no longer considered a war, but a police action. Police actions are legitimated not by their size or character, but by the nature and circumstances of the UN mandate.

It is interesting that in March of 2003, pacifists around the world were actively demonstrating against the United States military action in Iraq. But that was not the main issue that concerned the national governments hotly debating the issue in the UN corridors. The issue was whether the UN would authorize the United States attack. For most of the delegates, the issue of the future relevance of the UN Security Council in issues of war and peace transcended the immediate questions of whether to use force to end an obnoxious dictatorial regime.

On balance, this is a healthy development. Nothing in the history of the evolution of human societies suggests that a viable future world order can be achieved entirely through peaceful means. There will have to be recourse to military action when the conflicts that threaten global stability stubbornly defy any peaceful solution. Pacifists act in the finest humanitarian traditions of our species, but there are going to be many occasions over the next several generations when they will simply have to be overruled. There will be times when the world cannot wait upon protracted negotiations, and some kind of military action will be necessary. A critical issue will always be whether the action is taken in a way that strengthens or weakens the UN's authority.

CONCLUSIONS

As an American, I have grown up favoring democratic over authoritarian methods. As an observer of the world scene throughout the decolonization era, I have learned to doubt the capacity of any one nation, no matter how high-minded and idealistic, to tell some other society, with an utterly different culture, exactly how it should develop. As a realist, I have seen how power corrupts, and see no ready answer to the ancient question: "Yes, but who guards the guardians?"

For all these reasons I deplore the course the neoconservatives have set for my country. But the most important reason of all is that the world urgently needs a new world order that is based on the rule of law, backed up by broad acceptance of global ethical standards.

The people who will lead humanity in the next couple of generations need to have some kind of idea where they want to be heading, and they need to be able to communicate this idea to those who follow them. Pandit Nehru had a vision for an India riven by regionalism and caste, a vision for a united, secular, progressive country that could play a large and respected role on the world stage. He made some serious mistakes, but they were less important in the long run than his vision. That vision still survives, and still defines the essence of the Indian nation. Similarly, present and future world leaders need to communicate the vision of a unified, secular, global society to national governments everywhere, and to the people in them. Humankind needs to dream a little, and imagine a future, better world. Imagination, after all, is central to the first big bang of the human mind that occurred about fifty thousand years ago. Now it is time for us to imagine on a new scale and pull ourselves out of present chaos into something better.

NOTES

1. Cambridge Scientific Abstracts, http://www.csa.com/hottopics/ern/01jul/overview.html.

2. Technically, the gag rule applies only to US population assistance funds used in foreign family-planning programs. In practice, NGOs customarily commingle their health funds, with the result that the gag rule also inhibits operations in such fields as HIV/AIDS and maternal health plans.

14.

Visions of a Future World Order

A ldous Huxley's *Brave New World* and George Orwell's *1984* were among the better-known efforts during the first half of the twentieth century to conjure up pictures of a future world order. The two differed, but each provided a disturbing outline of a future totalitarian society in which the government has a monopoly over the production and dissemination of information. The "dystopias" they portrayed reflected a growing fear that modern science, and particularly modern techniques of communication, could make it possible for a few oligarchs to exercise total control over a large mass of people.

It's conceivable that some such outcome could represent the next major stage in the evolution of human society. There is ample precedent in human history for sytems based on rule of the many by the few. The old kingdoms and empires were usually run by a relatively small collection of nobles and priests, who maintained control over a largely ignorant and unlettered populace through conditioning and coercion. The late Soviet empire under Stalin demonstrated that control of the media, backed up by powerful instruments of coercion, can keep a large population in line, even in modern times. We cannot assume that some such concentration of power does not await our descendants.

In fact, human society as a whole is steering a tricky course between the Scylla of global anarchy and the Charybdis of totalitarianism based on mind control through the media. If we crash into Scylla, our societies will collapse, while if we veer too far in the other direction, our minds will become paralyzed.

Our goal should be the middle way, a future world order that is democratic and humane, secular and progressive. This is quite possible, provided the more important nation-states of our era remain willing to work out solutions to problems of mutual concern through a process of consultation and compromise. The intense opposition of many nations to President Bush's determination to invade Iraq unilaterally, if necessary, was based on the fact that on the crucially important issue of peace and war he was unwilling to compromise. These states saw Bush's determination to go it alone if necessary as a dangerous precedent leading the world away from the democratic world order they were trying to create, and toward one based on the alternative principle that might makes right.

The principle of democracy is crucially important, but it is important to define that concept broadly. Democracy can take many forms. It isn't enough to declare a country democratic because it has had an election. Elections can be rigged, or can misfire. The true hallmark of a functioning democracy is a tendency or impulse to move away from instruments of coercion toward acceptance of the rule of law, backed up by a generally accepted body of ethical principles. When the trend is in the other direction, toward increased reliance on instruments of coercion to maintain the group's integrity, democracy recedes and totalitarianism threatens. President Bush's administration is clearly moving in the direction of increased measures of coercion on the domestic front, using the threat of terrorism and the attack of 9/11 as justification.

Beyond the immediate problems of the Bush administration's behavior, however, what principles can we adduce as guidelines, as we reflect on the kind of world order we would like our descendants to enjoy? It is all very well to define that world order as "democratic and humane, secular and progressive," but can we be a bit more specific? This is a topic that merits far more discussion than it is currently receiving. I would like to suggest a couple of principles here, diversity and human rights, that I would accord priority in any effort to sketch out a specific vision of a future world order.

WHY DIVERSITY?

The evolutionary perspective central to this book strongly suggests that if our descendants are to enjoy a better life than we do, one where one's future is secure and one's creativity has ample opportunity to develop, then the global framework of the times has to accommodate a lot of diversity. That implies both diversity between geographic regions, and a multiplicity of coexisting social groups within each region, including power sharing between different levels of authority. This is not the kind of structure one expects to grow out of a process of subjugation of many peoples by a powerful few. It is, however, precisely what one might expect from an evolutionary process proceeding by increments, from one small step to the next.

Why diversity? Because a diverse society is more adaptable, in the long run, than a society in which everyone is dragooned into a single mode. People are people because they are creative, and no two minds are creative in exactly the same way. Our ancestors survived and then flourished and finally conquered the earth because there was usually some individual or group that thought a little outside the box in times of crisis, and came up with a winning solution. And now that we've conquered the earth we have to figure out what we are going to do with it. That is at least as big a challenge, and will demand at least as much thinking outside the box.

Why diversity? Because the planet itself is diverse. It is big, living spaces vary, and the ways people adapt to them vary. Human populations are much too diverse to be forced into a drab conformity. Witness the failure of Mao's "Great Leap Forward." Regimes that demand that the individual conform to a fixed model are inherently weaker than those that thrive with diversity. They do well for a while, perhaps, but they are inherently brittle.

Why diversity? Because it is beautiful, and pleasing to the senses, while conformity is dull, and can even be ugly. We aren't rational all the time, and there is something about the way the human mind works that can feel awe, even reverence, in the face of nature's marvelous diversity. As we grow toward a sense that all humanity is one big society, we can also grow in our ability to experience joy and even reverence at the marvelous diversity that our fellow humans have created, in the mental world we all share.

The principle of diversity has solid implications for us, as we pick our way through the minefield of contemporary problems, looking for solutions. Here are some ways the principle can be applied, when we think about the long-range future:

1. *Regional Diversity:* The future world order should consist of regionally defined entities, which often but not necessarily reflect today's political map of the world. Each such entity should draw on its unique historical and cultural roots to shape its own personality. There should be a worldwide ethical bias against attempts to homogenize everybody. Pride in one's particular region or culture or country can tap the wellsprings of human altruism. At present, this kind of loyalty often stands in the way of a newer ethic of loyalty to humanity as a whole, but this isn't necessarily the way it has to be. Our ancestors have added new levels of loyalty without destroying the older ones; I see no reason why our descendants cannot accomplish this once again.

2. *Layers, and the Federal Principle:* Multiethnic states, notably the United States, set the pattern here. We have seen that large countries that include many regional and cultural groups work best when those groups are recognized as legitimate and are empowered to wield authority in specified areas. Even the most harmonious world order we can imagine will need subgroups within the larger entity, of various sizes and shapes, that meet particular needs and that operate at levels reflecting the different layers of altruism we have acquired over the millennia.

3. *Freedom of Choice, by Countries as Well as Individuals:* In any world order based on democratic principles, different regions and different countries should be free to develop whatever cultural and ethical patterns and constraints they want to, as long as they do not violate the global authority's laws regarding matters of vital concern to everyone. That is,

they should not violate basic principles of human rights. They should not be allowed to develop weapons of mass destruction or fight their neighbors. They should not commit genocide. They should not grab more than their share of nonrenewable or finite resources, or pollute the global environment beyond prescribed limits. But within these and similar limits, they should be free to adopt whatever ideologies, value systems, and social and economic policies they want.

4. *Mobility:* This is a relatively long-term goal, rather than an immediately applicable principle like the first three. It can only be applied fully when the world has achieved a level of material prosperity sufficient to meet everyone's basic needs, and when global population levels have stabilized. Once those conditions have been largely achieved, however, the mobility principle can provide the key to reconciling individual freedom with the kinds of regional and national free choice I have just described. Any individual should be allowed to move to any region or country and resettle there. If he or she wants a large family and lives in a place that has a two-child rule, for example, that person should be able to move to another country with a more liberal attitude toward reproduction. That country might have a lower standard of living, but the individual would be free to sort out conflicting wants and select what on balance was the most suitable option. In other words, the world of the future might resemble a kind of supermarket offering a selection of legal codes and ethical structures, with people staying where they were born if it suited them, or moving on.

UNIVERSAL RESPECT FOR BASIC HUMAN RIGHTS

The world order of the future will only function harmoniously, and in a democratic fashion, if there is a prevailing belief in the principle of universal human rights. At present that principle coexists uneasily with the atavistic, instinctive impulse most people still have to regard individuals and groups as being either with "us" or with "them." Those falling into the "them" category are seen as less equal, less deserving of humane treatment, than people in the in-group. Ethnocentrism and even a touch of xenophobia still lurk in the inner recesses of most of our minds. Is this an essential part of our human nature, part of our genetic makeup? Is there anything we can do about it?

I believe the answer is yes, it is part of our nature, and yes, we can do something about it. There is plenty of precedent, as discussed in earlier chapters. The trick is to retain the old loyalties while subsuming them within the big tent of a new and larger sense of the in-group. The hostility toward outsiders that is inherent in any sense of "us versus them," at any level, becomes translated from latent hostility to a more benign rivalry. Soccer fans passionately want their team to win, but only exceptionally do they boil out of the bleachers and beat up the fans of the other team. When that does happen, it is taken as an aberration, and everyone chides them for their bad manners. Manners, in other words, has taken over as a mediator of intergroup competition, replacing outright conflict—except in truly exceptional cases.

As long as there is a possibility of rivalry leading to conflict, it is part of our shared human nature to demonize the rival group. When the rivalry exists in more benign form, within the ambit of a larger sense of community, demonization either doesn't occur at all, or is so transformed that it is rendered harmless.

One way to get national and ethnic rivalries subsumed within the big tent of a global humanism is to work on the tendency to demonize. Both familiarity with the person or group being demonized, and an understanding of motives, will undercut the demonization urge. Television and other media exposure to people and conditions in faraway places can and often does play a useful role here. So does travel. But the most important single factor is leadership. Pandit Nehru set the tone for India. There must be leaders on the world stage who are able and willing to do a similar job now, for the world as a whole. The best place to start would be

Washington, capital of the surviving superpower. The Bush administration has not measured up. The world can only hope that a successor administration will see the world, and the United States' role in it, in a different light.

CONCLUSION

Nothing in the future is inevitable, but the kind of future world we would like our descendants to enjoy is achievable.

15.

On the Importance
of Being Human

A ll through this book we've been examining the growth of social structures, and the evolution of ethical guidelines within those structures. The whole approach has been based on the theory of evolution. We are where we are today because of a gradual accretion, over many millennia, of social workarounds and spandrels that helped people cooperate more efficiently. The successful ones ended up being incorporated in the perceived wisdom of our ancestors. Our ethical structures evolved, along with other parts of our culture, in the direction of greater fitness with a constantly changing environment.

But are we missing something? Take my analogy comparing a human society, which encloses and defines an in-group of people, to an architectural structure, which encloses and defines a given space with outer walls and a roof. You can develop the analogy by comparing the inner partitions and floors with divisions between subgroups that maintain distinct identities within the overall society, at various levels. But this is still a dry and utilitarian construct. How about the furnishings? How about the rugs on the floors, the pictures on the walls, the furniture? How about the meals prepared in the kitchens and served in the dining areas, and the music, and the libraries full of books? There's a lot more to the architecture of human society than four walls and a roof.

When you look at the totality of the world of mental constructs that we and our ancestors have built, it's obvious that there's a lot more to being human than just being clever at social engineering. How does a strictly utilitarian approach account for the many different ways people in different societies express creativity, or derive pleasure, or perceive beauty? How about the hundreds of forms of religious practices different groups use to engender feelings of awe and wonder? Are we agnostics sure that our dry answers to the arguments of the pious are all that complete? Yes, we can be certain, as I stated in the first chapter, that our faith in a process called evolution holds up better under rational analysis than their faith in some unexplainable and unverifiable force—but do we really understand all the dark corners of the human mind that encourage and reinforce religious convictions? And if we did, would we perhaps conclude that that "great divide" I talked about earlier wasn't that unbridgeable after all?

In Kathmandu Valley they celebrate a variety of holidays and festivals. Some are celebrated all over the valley, but many others are particular to just one town or village. In one town they'll erect a kind of flagpole, elsewhere they'll drag a huge creaky vehicle around, and in another the young men will all get tipsy and throw colored powder on each other. The outstanding common feature is that everybody gets together and has a good time.

I used to find out where and when these festivals occurred, then visit them and sense the joy while taking a picture or two. I was a little worried that I was intruding where I didn't belong and would be resented. And indeed there was a little of that reaction at first. But pretty soon I became recognized and any trace of resentment vanished. The fact that I was actually having a good time with them was noticed and made all the difference. Word got up the line that I was a sympathizer, not a patronizer. It actually made a difference in the kind of rapport I was able to establish with high government officials and other leaders.

I guess I'm just lucky, growing up as the son of a prodigiously scholarly anthropologist and exposed from my earliest youth to an eclectic view of cultural variations around the world. I have always been curious about foreigners and their different ways. It never occurs to me to be afraid when confronting people whose culture is very different from mine, and while aspects of their culture sometimes strike me as distasteful, I don't feel superior, or assume that I'm right and the others are wrong. I feel refreshed, informed, and invigorated, the way one is supposed to feel when reading a good book.

The whole social evolution of our species has been based on the "us versus them" principle, so I shouldn't be surprised if relatively few people share my eclectic curiosity. Most of us still view foreigners through a moral lens refracted in accordance with the ethical guidelines we grew up with. We think of ourselves as tolerant, but in our hearts there's still some of that "us versus them" sense lurking, just a touch of cultural apartheid. We are still in transit, still at an interim stage in a gradual shift in our basic attitudes toward "foreigners." We are only apprentices in the grand task of learning to be genuinely tolerant.

People are disposed to be kind and decent to people they know. With the information age upon us, we are all getting to "know" each other. Despite all the conflict and commotion around us, the prospects for a broad-based attitudinal shift, in the direction of internalized respect and even affection for everyone everywhere, have never been better. This shift will take hold only on a generational time scale, but as it gathers momentum, it will become the transformational element that will propel our descendants into a new and more harmonious global society.

Believe me, when we find ourselves completely comfortable with foreign manners and customs, we shall have become fit for citizenship in a new world. And we shall discover that this new world is full of marvels and delights we never imagined when we were locked within the narrow confines of the nation we were born into. All things will become possible. And many of them will actually happen.

But first, the people of the United States of America must decisively reject the siren call of unilateralism based on American military preeminence. Destiny lies in leading the nations of the world out of nationalism and into a humanistically inspired globalism. The high road is leading by example and persuasion, the low road by coercion. The low road leads nowhere. The high one is the one my country must follow, starting now.

Index